Are We There Yet?

ENLIGHTENMENT FOR BUSY PEOPLE

Marcie Anderson

BALBOA.
PRESS

A DIVISION OF HAY HOUSE

Balboa Press books may be ordered through booksellers or by contacting:

Balboa Press
A Division of Hay House
1663 Liberty Drive
Bloomington, IN 47403
www.balboapress.com
1 (877) 407-4847

Print information available on the last page.

ISBN: 978-1-5043-7152-0 (sc)
ISBN: 978-1-5043-7153-7 (e)

Balboa Press rev. date: 12/28/2016

Contents

Prologue

If you have ever felt alone in this life, I can tell you, you are not alone. If you have ever questioned the events that happen in your life, please, have faith there is a higher power that's got your back. And just as surely, if you've experienced a strong intuitive *knowing* and gone with your hunch to a positive end, I can tell you, it was not a fluke.

So what is operating in you or *out there*? Are we in control of our destinies, or are we merely at the will of a God or the whims of fortune? I believe we are, as humans, quite extraordinary. Each of us is a highly functioning creature who will experience many opportunities to learn and grow. We feel, we experience, we react, we enjoy love or feel the pain of loneliness. We achieve goals and suffer defeats.

We have complex relationships with family, lovers, friends, enemies, colleagues, neighbors and even our pets. We desire healthy, loving, lasting relationships and yet we send out mixed signals due to past heartbreak, misunderstandings, karmas and the seeping in of our emotional challenges.

So why is it that there is a shared, deeply profound lack of lasting happiness and satisfaction in our lives? How can we make positive changes in our lives that stick? Is it even possible? How many of us truly have a sense of inner peace, calm and clarity?

I invite you to tag along with me on a journey of Awakening the Soul. This journey does not come with a complimentary soft drink and a mini bag of pretzels, but feel free to grab what you need. We will start the journey through the lens of my life, when, as a wee young lass of five years old. You'll laugh and you'll learn, you'll relate to some of my tales, and you'll be coaxed inward to remember and reflect upon some of your own experiences. In these moments, I would like you to stop and consider if you have the room for wonder, appreciation, imagination, courage, acceptance and maybe even forgiveness. The goal of our journey is to experience a profound heart opening, healing, and awakening within you. So on this trip you can leave the packing, the long lines, and U.S. Customs behind. You are safe, you are home, so kick back and know you are loved beyond what you know is love.

Sri Kaleshwar

Before going any further, I want to acknowledge my teacher, my guru, Sri Kaleshwar. As a modern spiritual master, Kaleshwar is in the lineage of Shirdi Sai Baba, Jesus Christ, Babaji, Ramakrishna Paramhamsa, Mother Mary and Ramana Maharishi. He was born in 1973, to a typical Hindu family in Southern India and on March 15, 2012, he took *mahasamadhi* and left his physical body. During his brief life, he demonstrated miraculous and direct experiences of the Divine to his students and devotees around the world. He was known for a vast number of humanitarian projects in Andhra Pradesh, South India, and shared the knowledge and taught practices from the ancient palm leaf manuscripts practiced by Jesus Christ of Nazarene and the Maharishis of India.

I struggle with words to describe my brief years with Kaleshwar. When we met, he was a slight young man who'd never traveled West. I was a young, defiantly independent sports model living in Los Angeles, yet I felt as if I was a lump of coal, transformed by his grace and divine presence. I experienced my years with him as a stripping away of all I knew to be true, much like the peeling back of petals of a rose, to discover a primordial truth and a slow and sometimes painful reconstruction of the person I am today.

Kaleshwar was a living saint, an avatar, and a spiritual master with a lightening quick sense of humor. He taught his "dense" Western students with an infectious smile, and offered pure ancient knowledge and healing wisdom. His teachings would often bypass the minds of his students, and reach our subconscious to find a resting place deep in our souls. Indeed, Kaleshwar was perfection in an alchemy of enlightenment, spiritual knowledge, humanity and humor. He accomplished this with the grace of a gentle swan and the ferocity of a wild tiger.

As a child, I was not a stellar student, and had very little patience for the mundane. My school teachers failed to inspire and engage me to get me, and my Catholic upbringing brought me only frustration. But with Kaleshwar, I was a junkie. I couldn't get enough. My only frustration was that hunger, sleep and occasional illness prevented my studies with him to continuously thrive while practicing and living in India. I humbly *pranam* to Kaleshwar for his kindness and support during this lifetime and the for lifetimes that came before, and the lifetimes to come. He was an amazing teacher, had patience beyond human capacity, and had a knack of not speaking one word that was useless. He was impeccable. Even now, in meditation or in a dream, my soul will recall a snippet of a conversation or interaction between us and just like he had said many countless times, "you need to read again my talks, you need to think more deeply our conversations, because there is that much depth to the meanings...they are many layers deep."

It is my intention and prayer that you, who are reading this now, continue to read the entire book. No skipping ahead to the last couple pages, although I know you'll be tempted. This is a process. It is my desire for you that you come away with a solid shift in your process of awakening, or at least your desire to do so. There is no price tag you can put on gaining and having consistent, authentic inner peace and true satisfaction in your life. The sheer power of an open heart, one that can be healed of past wounds and misunderstandings, and one that has the ability to give and receive a high Divine quality of love is beyond any other type of power. It is immortal and it is healing like nothing else on the planet. The power of forgiveness will rock your world. When you can arrive at true forgiveness you will not treat yourself poorly and it will be next to impossible to throw negative and hurtful thoughts at someone else without first feeling a deep connection to them and a compassion for his or her condition. The rich, unparalleled Divine Love of The Divine Mother is something every soul needs to experience, to remember. Once you have that, there is nothing higher or more important. And last, humor and God are twins. Humor and God are in cahoots together to not only shake us out of our own personal small bubbles of ego existence in order to truly wake up, but to make sure that in the waking up we have a blast, we can laugh at ourselves, and that we get over ourselves already.

> *"When we have the ability to receive the silence in our heart, then automatically the purification of the silence gives a part of the highest information."*

> \- Sri Kaleshwar

Awakening Through The Elements

We will dive deep into our awakening and relate to our life experiences by way of the Five Elements - Earth, Fire, Sky, Water and Air. Through each of these elements, we will peel away our inherited beliefs, our perceptions, our reactions, karmas, and the stories we tell ourselves and others about who we are. We will uncover our truth and learn to trust our inner voice and intuition with greater confidence. And, if done consciously, this exercise will allow for a more profound natural connection to be revealed.

While studying and practicing in India for many years, the ancient spiritual knowledge revealed to me that everything in this Creation is made up of and is under the control of the Five Elements. There is nothing in this Creation where the Five Elements do not exist. Countless ancient traditions and civilizations have pointed to the greatness, profundity and perfection of Nature. Nature is perfection. All the world's remedies are here. Kaleshwar would often say, "Nature is the right, perfect teacher." It was through the combination of my

Fire element, my will power and my passion to know the truth, and my sheer stubbornness, as well as the purification practices and meditation processes given to me by Kaleswhar, which resulted in a silence and peace deep within me. But it didn't stop there. That was just a warming up of my engine. I began to have experiences that grew quickly and did not leave me. They built upon themselves, one upon another, revealing to me that I had become reconnected and reintroduced to the peace and information inside of the Five Elements. It was the most satisfying feeling of a coming home.

This is just one of the vast number of gifts I received while going through my many years of this intense process. I had been playing hide and seek with myself and finally my drama had ended. Thank you, God! It was exhausting. I wanted to know the Truth, then help others in their search to know their truth too, why they are here in this lifetime, and find true and lasting peace. I know I kept hiding from myself and denying my intuition because I had not found the right answers, until I met my guru. I grew up feeling insecure and uncertain of a lot, and that I had no real peace in me. When I was able to re-connect to this vast and powerful inner silence, through the Five Elements and through the unbelievable patience and grace of my teacher, it felt like opening a vault with limitless amounts of energy and unconditional love. It was a process where layers and layers of doubt, fear, sadness, pain, anger, judgment and confusion were removed. This process required a lot of journaling, meditation, shedding of my ego and lots waterproof mascara.

> *Having a sadguru, you allow him to do whatever he wants to do in your life. 'He's my well-wisher. He is everything in my life. Let him do whatever he wants to do.' Then he can make the inner bliss grow in you very powerfully."*
>
> - Sri Kaleshwar

The Five Elements – The Forces of Nature

I have broken down conceptually, the Five Elements of Creation; Earth, Fire, Sky, Water and Air. Each element is a reflection or a section of my life. I have laid out a menu of reference for comparison of how each element represents specific segments of my life; happenings, epiphanies, struggles, sufferings, and victories. All of these have taken me from a shy, stuttering, cussing little girl with moxie, who experienced trauma, confusion, anger, loss, a sense of not belonging, and fear, sprinkled with chaos, to a grown, balanced, grounded and clear woman who moved from Oregon to Los Angeles, then to India for many years, who studied and practiced alongside a Spiritual Master, Avatar and Saint. I resurfaced back in the West after having gone through massive transformation, with having a lot to share, and of course, still with a fair share of moxie intact.

Earth

The earth has the strongest magnetic pull of all of the Five Elements. This can be a peaceful element or it can disturb, shake and crack like the experience of an earthquake. The earth has the capacity to create, sustain and destroy. It is difficult to always feel grounded, supported, and centered, much like it is difficult to always control our own earth element energy. When we are feeling stuck in life, we suffer from physical illness, or lack of sustained peace and balance. The water and fire elements help bring balance to this powerful element.

Fire

A fire can be mesmerizing, and still it burns, it destroys. Yet if you watch a fire, deep sensations of peace are experienced. It has the capacity to pull, to suck cosmic energy into itself to allow huge transformation. Fire creates heat, pressure, and the opportunity for growth and change, much like the sun. The fire element can represent anger, impatience, and frustration. Our goal is to balance the fire element energy through the use of the earth, air and water elements.

Sky

The sky is unbounded, endless, hopeful, expansive, all-encompassing. It is like a comfortable blanket that can never be taken away. To speak to the skies is to speak to God. Haven't you found yourself physically looking up at the sky when you are whole heartedly praying, or wanting to find an answer? By connecting deeply with the sky element, great peace and strong intuition is possible. In Eastern Indian traditions, the Sky element is believed to hold the infinite power of the angels.

Water

Nurturing, refreshing, purifying, peaceful and fulfilling. Just as there is rain that falls from the sky, and tears from our eyes, the water we drink keeps us alive and thriving. Water is the life liquid in the womb that creates a baby. The water element is how all living things on this planet have come into creation. The water element can also be the vehicle to bring great destruction like a tsunami, so that a new creation can be born. When our water element is out of balance, it can bring on strong feelings of anger or depression symptoms. One way to balance our water element is through the earth element.

Air

The breath of life. Our creative thoughts. The monkey mind, our ceaseless, bouncing and relentless chatter. Creation and sustaining life. It is given to us in our first seconds of life and the last gift to be taken from us at death. Destruction through tornadoes or pure negative thoughts or words spoken. Beautiful, melodious healing through music and speaking about supernatural, Divine and loving topics. The fire and air elements can purely destroy or very powerfully create.

A Teacher By Any Other Name Is Still A Teacher

> *"A master is necessary to guide you until you know who you are. The real master is always living in you. You have to recognize that is the one truth."*

-Sri Kaleshwar

When you hear about the word "guru" is it off-putting? It certainly can be, especially in the West. But bear with me and perhaps overlay the term "Nature" wherever I use the term, "Guru." After all, other meanings for the term guru would be teacher, master, or qualified and skilled guide.

In our life, we've come across many teachers. Looking over the many teachers we've encountered, a few stand out over all the others, and when we've gained whatever lesson, whether it be a human lesson or a spiritual one, the teacher goes away. Job done. It is no different, that when we are calling out and crying for the right teacher to come into our lives, that he or she appears. Much like the phrase, "When the student is ready, the teacher will appear." But is there a limit to having a teacher? Yes. Throughout your personal soul journey you will come to the conclusion that Nature is your true teacher. Nature connects our soul to the immortal inner teacher - to Self. God. Goddess. The Divine Mother, Father, The Almighty, the Cosmic Universal Intelligence. That inner teacher is referred to in Eastern terminology as "Consciousness."

According to the vedic tradition, we are the luckiest to be born as a human being because only a human incarnation, equipped with all the bells and whistles, provides the fertile ground, potential, and abilities to reach God. The right and perfect tools to understand who we are, and to truly wake up is alive and well and available. The alarm clock is in our hands. *There is no battery required, but the clock is ticking.*

Soul Journey Exercises For Each Element

In this book, I will ask you to participate in your own self-inquiry, and to awakening through the Five Personal Steps, relating to each of the Five Elements. I will be with you every step of the way, but not literally because that would be impossible, expensive and well, weird. The exercises will be laid out at the end of each chapter, but for now I will let you in on what you will need to complete each chapter and to truly embark upon this Soul Journey.

I will guide you with how to Create a Sacred Space. I will offer a few insightful questions to help ignite your deepest truth and inspiration to "look for the lesson in the experience." I will do my best to help you Find the Humor in all of life, even in the darkest corners you may find yourself. The gift I will give is the Divine Glue to make your Soul Journey a success and flourish through the Art of Meditation and Silence

Action Items/Fun Chores

1. Let's go shopping
2. How to create a Sacred Space
3. Looking for the Lessons in the Experience
4. Laughter is the best Soul Medicine
5. Creating the Silence (making it all work and last)

You will need to do a little work, and you will get to enjoy a little play. I will not trick you into doing any unnecessary housework, though you will need to do a little shopping! Yes, part of becoming Enlightened is knowing when to go shopping, turns out. You will need to purchase the following items, but there is a slight catch. You will need to be in a peaceful, receptive space in order to bring your awareness to these items that will become treasures in your life.

A Soul Journal

Try to choose a color you love, or one that has a beautiful quote on the cover, or maybe the texture just feels good and comfortable in your hands. You will only use this journal for this process, and for any epiphanies, dreams, or messages related to this book and exercises will go into this Soul Journal. This will become a powerful, insightful and freeing tool that you will revisit from time to time after the completion of your Soul Process.

Your Special Mantra

An individual's right and perfect mantra holds a specific frequency, that repeated many times, will activate your personal vibration, unlocking your Soul Code. It is a system that is thousands upon thousands of years old. Once this activation takes place, you become open to receive divine knowledge, which becomes your soul's unique intelligence. The combination of this mantra, your intention and your attention to the Five Elements will powerfully affect not only you, but those around you, and well beyond, stretching out to the infinitude of this universe.

A Special Space

This is very important. In my case, I have a special area in my home delegated as Sacred. I set up a small table with photos of Kaleshwar and other Divine Souls that are dear to my heart, with tea lights (white) and fresh flowers (mostly roses). I recommend you clean it by wiping it down every few days with pure Rose Water. The vibrations that will be created through such loving attention will soon affect you and all others in your home in a highly positive way. For some, you might struggle with what photos or images to place on your table or meditation space, and I get it. I advise you to search for an image of an Angel that opens your heart, or maybe it is a breathtaking display of a waterfall or a sunset. It's all Divine, it's Nature. It is best to find an image or photo of a Divine Soul and to be able to look into their eyes.

Candles or Incense

Try to choose a specific color to your candle(s) and a distinct fragrance to your incense. You may want to use this color /fragrance through each of the Elements, though you are welcome to change colors and fragrances at will. For instance, for the Earth Element, maybe you choose green to represent the life growing on the planet represented as the grass and trees and bushes, or maybe it is a blue/green blend. Have fun, trust your intuition and enjoy this process of treating yourself. These mindfully selected items will actually feed your soul positive energy that will build upon itself.

Fresh Flowers

Whether you pick these from your own garden, or if you hand pick a bundle from your local market, make sure they are flowers you love, and the more fragrant the better. I would suggest you choose either roses, jasmine or sunflower, but any flower you love will work. You do not need to buy an entire new bundle each day since most flowers last about a week, but please be mindful to make sure they are peppy and alive.

Creating the right vibrations

Whenever possible, it is best to have no electricity, but if it is necessary, make it a gentle light; nothing overhead or harsh. Candle light is best. Do not allow any other distractions in your space such as a blaring tv, loud conversations, etc. If you prefer music then choose melodious, gentle music that will play softly in the background. There are recorded mantras specific to meditation that are helpful in creating the right vibrations as well. Your aim for each time you mindfully sit to read and journal is to create and protect your vibrations and your sacred space. Remember, you are intending to create and invite pure Divine vibrations. We all need to touch upon the silence, because it is in the pure silence that we can hear our soul.

"Every person has good and negative qualities-try to take the positive always. If you keep going on the negative your life will turn as a negative."

-Sri Kaleshwar

Chapter One

Earth Element

"The highest energy is Faith. Faith is gained through meditation, and in meditation the soul connects to the highest energy. Connecting to God."

-Sri Kaleshwar

I Was Born Ready

According to Mom, the fact that she had any children at all is a miracle. She claims when she had to go under the knife for a complete hysterectomy after the birth of her fourth child, my youngest brother, the doctor told her post-surgery, it looked liked she had only menstruated a handful of times in her entire lifetime. This was of course back in the day when the medical staff may have come to work a bit tipsy, hung over, or a combination of the two, so I don't know who to believe in this case. But nonetheless, there I was, the only girl out of four children, and third in the pecking order. I was born premature and jaundice, and to this day I cannot for the life of me wear anything yellow or orange. I had to stay in the hospital from the time I was born for a total of three weeks. At birth I only weighed in a at a whopping 4.5 pounds, so basically I was born a large plantain. To this day, bananas repel me. Mom, an RN, said she had me baptized three times during this period of three weeks because she said, "I didn't think you were going to make it." Not a confidence booster, but I took it to heart. By the time I got released from the hospital I wasn't much better off and had dropped down to 3 lbs., which meant I had to be fed every two hours around the clock. Well, the magic liquid and the three Holy Spa treatments worked. I not only pulled through, but came out of it stronger and quite the fighter.

The running joke in the family was that I was named after the family dog, Max. Max began with an "M" and so did "Marcie." My brothers, all "Bs" - Brett, Bruce and Bart - meant I was special…at least, that's what I told myself and still do. Our dog Max was cute, a fast runner, and was well-liked, so I took well to the M-named pairing.

I grew up in a smallish town in Oregon in a modest house on the corner of a dead end street. Ironically, my life could have developed into somewhat of a dead end, had it not taken a rather intense and unexpected turn. A turn so great nobody could have predicted.

Raised Catholic, my parents made us kids go to church every Sunday until we were old enough to rebel or get good at faking we were too ill to attend. There were many times that merely bribing us with post-church doughnuts would make us crawl out of bed, magically cured of our feigned ailments. A good maple bar and an "Amen" can be hard to pass up.

I grew up part tomboy, part girlie girl. I was the badass on the softball field, on the track and volleyball court with painted nails and french braids with ribbons flying behind, but with a mouth like a truck driver. As long as I could keep them hidden from my brothers, I had a few Barbie dolls that I loved because I could play with their long hair and braid it until my hands were cramped. I may have initiated a few inappropriate moments between GI Joe and Barbie, but nothing was on film in those days so for the record, I am innocent. But Barbies, and playtime and underwear clad doll tea parties didn't last long. For one reason, my brothers found my doll stash and ripped their heads off, then proceeded to throw them outside the second story bathroom window into the massive holly bush, never to be seen again. The new home owners have no idea the holly bush is actually a Barbie-head, graveyard.

There was another reason that my world at the age of three and a half, and any sense of normal playtime, abruptly had the wind taken out of its sails. Like a thick and sickening black cloud that seeped into our home, in 1971, my family received the terrible news that my oldest brother, Brett, had been diagnosed with leukemia at the age of seven and a half. The innocence and joyful dynamics of the family as a whole changed in an instant, like the flick of a switch. Like having the wind knocked out of you, you are left gasping for air, clutching your stomach, dazed in disbelief. I quickly noticed a strong shift in the behavior of my parents, not only with one another, but also towards us children, individually and collectively. There was a fear, a pain, a heaviness, a low-ceiling feeling, a deep sadness. Even Max felt it, as did our cat, Oreo. Our lives were now all about walking on eggshells but putting on a strong face for Brett, for the public, for ourselves and for each other. An awkward and strange nauseousness came into all our lives that day, lodging deeply in our guts. It was a feeling that would take many years to subside, and for some of us, was a feeling that never left.

I remember Mom being the designated parent to drive my oldest brother Brett to his chemo and radiation appointments in her green 'Volare' with pleather seats, the cloud of smoke from mom's Marlboro Reds, and the air freshener hanging from the rear view mirror that made no difference whatsoever. Dad held down the fort at his emerging accounting practice in town and did his best to manage our family 'balls'. Throughout it all, I remember watching the strange metamorphosis of my brother, when his fair complexion of soft golden peach turned to a whitish gray. His tiny body developed a bloated tummy, and his hair, once a soft golden brown, began to fall out in clumps. At times he would pick at his fingernails until they eventually just fell off. I remember vividly the times I just couldn't stomach looking at him at all because his suffering and pain made me want to be sick – I loved him so much.

My brother began to look like an entirely different person. But thank God we all had a sense of humor...especially him at this time. I think he stuck his toxic fingernails in an envelope and mailed them off to one of my parents friends as a joke, because that was his idea of funny. I am not so sure the family who received these took it very well. It was one less Christmas card we would receive from that family from then on.

I remember his smiles through the grimaces and strain in his eyes as he was being dosed, poisoned by chemo and radiation. I remember the smell of Mylanta, the chalky, milky, stinky thick white medicine he would do his best to choke down to try and alleviate his massive nausea. He drank Gatorade to try and boost his minerals and electrolytes. He was always sick from these intense sessions, and would have help getting cleaned up again by Mom; and at times I would assist her. The thin chalky Mylanta would remain defiantly around the corners of his mouth, even after being lovingly wiped down by warm wash cloths. Brett would have cotton balls held down by white medical tape where he'd been stuck by another needle for yet another blood test. The nurses drew bunny ears and faces on the cotton and tape to try and make him smile. No doubt it was hard for them to stick him yet again to draw more blood. Brett would let them do it every time with a weak smile, and he'd lend an artists direction to the slightly evolved bunny face to help provide the nurses with some levity. Maybe he knew it would make them feel better for having to put him through yet another blood draw.

There were countless trips to the clinic and the doctor, and Brett had so much nausea and pain that he had to begin to manage this stage as it became his new normal. What I noticed as something consistent, was that he'd always seem to manage a smile throughout all of this torture, as if feeling more compassion towards those administering all these painful tests. I remember feeling this tirade of emotions all at once as I struggled within myself to understand what this was and what was happening, and why to my big brother? These waves of emotional turmoil would come and go, and that became my new normal. I wrestled with wanting to just ball my eyes out and hug the cancer out of him, and at the same time, I had fear that I would hurt his delicate body, or that I would catch it just as simply as a common cold, if I were too close to him. I tried cussing it out of him a few times, as I screamed into my teddy bears, to no avail. There was no point of reference for me and as a family we did not sit down and discuss all our questions, feelings and fears around this. We were no Walton family in that sense.

Brett was aware that his group of friends from grade school slowly began to dwindle one-by-one and he didn't understand why. I remember him crying and asking my parents, "Why…why…why don't they want to come over and play with me anymore?" Many times I would overhear these conversations from around the corner and I would begin to cry too, at the additional emotional pain he had to suffer. Wasn't the leukemia enough? Now his friends had to be asses? At times I would look out our large living room window and see familiar neighbors and Brett's friends as they'd look into our home as they sheepishly passed by as if hoping not to see Brett, but also wanting to maybe give a quick wave or smile if they did. They were noncommittal and I didn't like that about them. Most just walked past with their heads down as if suddenly mesmerized by the sidewalk until they got far enough away that they felt safely out of sight. But I watched them, my face pressed up against the farthest edge of the corner of the window, making breath fog on the glass. Each time they would look back just as they felt the relief of feeling out of sight, and the coast was clear, but they didn't understand I was invested in my post. I called them bad names under my breath and would say a prayer they'd step in a fresh pile of dog crap.

Brett was as an artist and could paint from memory. He would sit patiently for hours, meticulously working at some creation with a striking resemblance, though he had no prior artistic training or direction. He'd look at a picture of a small wood duck or mallard, both the male and female, then he'd paint them on a clean block of wood, getting so intricate that he'd use a toothpick to paint in the details of their feathers and eyes. He'd put together model airplanes and tanks, pimp them out in full decal and paint detail, then hang the airplanes precariously by thumb tack and fishing line at precarious angles on the ceiling in his bedroom to resemble in flight fighting tactics. Who knows, maybe he enjoyed a small contact high from the toxic glue that made him feel a bit better than he did most of the time. If so, *awesome*. It didn't seem real that he should possess such raw talent, patience and discipline, not to mention such courage, humor and playfulness, while fighting such a vicious illness. That got my attention in a strange way. Of all the ways one can be through such continuous pain and such uncertainty, not to mention those around him who had difficulty managing their own emotions, Brett was remarkably even keeled, gentle, insightful…and a rascal, which I loved. It made me consider, did he know something we didn't know?

A couple of years passed and my brother's health ebbed and flowed. His blondish hair came and went and now his hair had grown in thicker, darker and wavy. He looked handsome and I remember trying to picture him when he would be older and healthy, and wishing he'd find a great girlfriend, and how she would become like a big sister. But those imaginings faded, and as his sickness progressed and the whitish-gray complexion and pain behind the smile in his eyes reminded me to stay in the moment. I remember thinking to myself, *is this still my same brother?*

As a family things stepped up a notch and we began going into the local clinic repeatedly to have blood drawn for various tests. Soon we found out all of these tests were so that the doctors could find a match to Brett's blood and marrow type, and the eligible one would become the donor of a bone marrow transplant surgical procedure. Back in 1975, this procedure was just emerging onto the blood cancer remedy scene. Mom told me later that I was a perfect match, as was my second oldest brother, and since he was older, they went with him as the donor.

A well known cancer research facility in Los Angeles was the closest option for the donor procedure, so my parents farmed my (healthy) brothers and me out to a neighbor just down the street, while Mom and Dad, with fear and hope rivaling their hearts and thoughts, traveled with Brett to southern California to begin the arduous process of this delicate and lengthy procedure. I remember the neighbors we stayed with were amazing, considering that they had three children of their own, taking in three more for many weeks to come was a tall order. I liked that there were two older girls to play with, and I got excited that I could braid their hair and show off my skills! But they were much older and more mature than me and when they got tired of letting me braid their hair, they'd drift off to their rooms to write in their diary about the boys they liked, or how much they wanted that new pair of San Francisco Riding Gear jeans. Perhaps the truth was, they were not braid worthy. Hard to say. The parents were strict and I don't remember a lot of laughter at their dining room table. This was a red flag. This troubled me. Absolutely no belching and certainly no farting allowed. My brothers and I were in unfamiliar, unchartered territory, and a bit spun out, really. No dog under the table to throw scraps to, either. What planet were we on? Who were these crazy-ass people?

It all seemed too quiet for me. I was used to my parents cussing and yelling, doors slamming, people falling down, food being tossed across the table, someone being made to laugh just as they took a gulp of milk so the milk would shoot out their nostrils, the dog barking and eating the poor cat's food, yet again. Indeed, this quiet and orderly place was alien to us. At breakfast, this mom would serve us corn flakes, warm milk, half a banana and prune juice before school. Prune juice! Every morning! For those of you who have never had the privilege of being made to drink prune juice, just know it looks and smells an awful lot like the brownish, pungent liquid that comes out of your back end if you've eaten too many prunes in the first place. I didn't see the logic in it. I was beginning to miss my parents badly, as well as Brett, my own bedroom, my teddy bears, church (because of donuts), my headless dolls the family dog, Max, and Oreo the cat, both of whom had to stay home alone.

Turquoise Was The Old Black

After a few months, it became time for my second oldest brother, Bruce, to make his way down to southern California to go through his round of the surgery as the bone marrow transplant donor to Brett. Now it was just my youngest brother, Bart and I at the somber prune juice breakfast table; our world seemed to continue to become smaller and smaller. I didn't like this feeling at all. I remember Bart and I would sneak into each other's beds at night just to cuddle each other. We were clinging to any and all love and familiarity we could get at this point. Finally, we were flown down to Los Angeles to join Mom and our brothers. Dad had to return back to his job, since he had been away for many weeks by this point. We all stayed in the patient/family apartments just off the medical campus. I remember seeing a lot of turquoise everywhere. Buildings, cars, appliances, clothes…to this day, I have a visceral reaction to the color! Most everything from the outside of the apartments to the scant, disturbing wall decor, to the plastic dusty flowers in their gaudy plastic dusty vases was turquoise or a faint shade thereof. I remember the elevators were loud and creepy. And it smelled like wet underwear, grocery store perfume, and stale cigarettes in the halls of these buildings. School work dwindled to 'just getting by' and managing through this intense time, although I do remember some tutoring from time to time to try and help us catch us up with our schoolwork requirements. But I really didn't care. My mind and thoughts were not at all on school.

Our life was simple. We were either at the hospital or we were in our little medical campus apartment. That was it. Television shows vacillated between Looney Tunes Cartoons and MASH. Going to "dinner" meant I could have all the Shirley Temples and maraschino cherries I wanted, but it also meant having to go through the buffet line at the bar during Happy Hour. I felt strange eyes on me as I picked at the snack food to fill my appetizer sized plate. I looked around and thought, "what were all of these weirdoes doing here" and "how come there is no chocolate or cookies?" What can I say, I wasn't *deep* I was a kid. This is a lame buffet line, bar or no bar. I thought of talking to the management but after getting a couple Shirley Temples in me, I calmed down. Although I loved my Shirley Temples, I found out later how terribly toxic those "cherries" are and I probably still have a few lodged in my intestines to this day. We were instructed by Mom to eat as much as we could. I chose the celery and carrot sticks, cherrie tomatoes, black and green olives, store bought assorted crackers made with shortening, and lots of ranch dressing. For mom, it meant eat some greasy chicken wings and watch her stuff her purse full of them to take back to the room for later. Well, later and greasy chicken wings never made much sense to me and in protest, never ate the cold ones from her purse. Once back to our apartment room, we showered to remove the lingering layers of cigarette smoke and cheap perfume out of our hair and skin, and put on fresh pajamas. To this day, mom still sneaks condiments and candy into her purse at restaurants. But no chicken wings, thank God. We were doing our best at making due and God bless Mom for holding it together for us kids, against so many odds. She was managing to the very best of her ability. Seriously, hats off to her.

Time passed and it was now the moment for the surgery. Dad returned to be with the rest of the family. We were on pins and needles and hours passed like months waiting for this procedure to be finished, and successfully. Finally, just minutes after the operating room doors opened and we received the news from one of the nurses, that both of my older brothers had come out of their delicate medical procedure, I remember watching the medical team emerge as if in slow motion, out the post-op doors looking tired, sweaty and relieved. They were walking down the hall slowly towards the front desk waiting area to report the good news, as if in a slow motion hero shot from a movie. When all of a sudden, as if shot out of a cannon, a nurse came out of the double doors yelling, "Doctor, the patient went into reaction!" I swallowed hard and my heart jumped. The small window of positive news and triumphant momentum lasted only a few seconds. I felt both suddenly paralyzed in fear and like I might be sick. For that moment all we could do as a family was pace and wait, then wait and pace. After a painfully long time, the doctor again walked out of the post-op room, wiping his forehead with the back of his hand. I had so many thoughts and scenarios torturing me as they were running through my mind, none of which were happy or positive. The doctor was nothing but a strange facial expression as he again walked towards us to give us the news. He looked fatigued, embarrassed and in awe all at the same time at what had just happened. My 'donor' brother had had a negative reaction to the anesthesia and had gone into hyperthermia. He had crashed hard and quickly as a result of the anesthesia and an allergic reaction to tetracycline, the antibiotic administered. But they were able to stabilize him and usher him into his own recovery after some time.

Doctors and nurses continued to rush past us, speaking in doctor talk that I couldn't understand, but sensed was not good. A few days later, the air seemed a bit easier to breathe, and hooray— my second oldest brother had recovered enough to scoot around the hospital hallways in a wheelchair tormenting the staff, demanding more popsicles. I exhaled hard, knowing that was a good sign and he was on the mend. And Brett's body had accepted the bone marrow transplant positively so he would now go into observation recovery, but in full blown ICU style. Whenever we would go into visit him in his room, we had to cover our shoes with paper booties, put on a gown and bad hair net looking paper head cover, a paper face mask and gloves. Thank God that look never made it to the runways of Milan, staying fashionable only in past-op rooms, meat packing plants, and the streets of Asia. This crucial time became more observation than recovery, and a long road that none of us thought we'd ever have to go down together.

A Paper Doll With an Attitude

Brett was a champ. He took his meds, ate his creepy jell-o, devoured the real food we snuck in for him, continued his light physical therapy, kept his IV in, and even spent some of his time sketching and painting. But he had no hair. Well he had hair, but only about 30 hairs randomly clinging on for dear life, as if each hair were in competition with each other. He was grayish white in complexion and had fingernails like faint, brittle glass. His lips always looked a bit chapped. He looked cooked, thirsty. He was very thin, but there remained a mischievous twinkle in his eyes and a sly grin at the corners of his mouth. His sense of humor was well intact. He still had his full-on rascal intact. No treatment of surgery could remove this! After his physical therapy sessions he'd toss his weights onto the floor knowing full well he was going to piss off his downstairs neighbor. He'd get a kick out of hearing a faint yell of protest from his neighbor, then he'd wait to watch a nurse's aide come knocking at his door, rushing in nervously to let him know he shouldn't do that again, as if apologizing for having to tell Brett this, yet again. He'd act coy, putting on his best acting performance, and apologize in her presence with a perfect poker face, but once she left, we'd all have a laugh about it. And of course, he'd do it again the next day.

Brett ended up being in the hospital in southern California from the time he was admitted to post-procedure for close to a year. The hospital was a busy place and a part of the staff were attendees, but were always assisted and supervised by the primary doctor or nurse to make sure small procedures of IV replacement, blood tests, bed pans, or general patient care and chart updates were handled professionally and properly. But there was this one time, this perfect storm moment that things did not go well for Brett. A resident intern came in to give my brother a shot, but no normal stick in the arm. No 'perfect storm' ends well. He came to give a very specific shot in the hip with a six inch needle in order to extract a smidgen of marrow to be tested. This was not your run of the mill poke in the hip with a needle. I was the only one in the room at the time, once again dressed from head to toe in stinky hospital paper over my clothing to assure my germ-freeness. I was tiny myself, so I looked like a roll of toilet paper with huge, scanning eyes.

I smelled a rat (and the rat was this adult dressed in paper garb like me) and I knew by the pit in my stomach that something was not right with this rat. My parents were doing anything else at the time; smoking, eating, crying, praying, hugging each other, making phone calls, etc. The intern looked at me and I noticed a nervousness and a shiftiness in his eyes. I didn't like that. My eyes narrowed, zeroing in on this guy. My Dad taught me that anyone who can't look you in the eyes directly is probably an asshole. My asshole radar was on high alert. I tried to lock in on him with my eyes in an evil stare but he wasn't having it. Brett's head doctor was not there with him. And no nurse. He was alone. But he had me. The attendee warned my brother that it might hurt a little as he had Brett roll over onto his side to prepare for the shot. He uncovered a small patch of my brother's side hip and rubbed it with an alcohol swab. I noticed already that this attendee's hands were shaking as he tore the plastic-foil-paper encasing to the sterile wipe. My heart rate began to increase as I stood beside my brother trying to look into his eyes to smile and comfort him for what was about to happen, but knew my eyes must have looked like full balloons. It's as if we both felt something very wrong was about to happen. Brett closed his eyes tightly. The attendee made his first attempt and missed. Brett winced and flinched, then let out a feeble yell. The attendee told Brett firmly he needed to be still as the attendee wiped at his forehead. There was a second attempt and Brett seemed to jump up off his bed a bit at the amount of pain this unskilled intern with darting eyes was forcing, and that was enough for me to know I needed to get my brother help. NOW. There was no time to run over to this rat and kick him in the nuts or bite his ankles. I yelled at him although muffled through my paper mouth covering, "Stop! You're hurting him!" I burst out the first doors that kept the main room sterile, then the outer doors into the hallway. I bolted down the hallway as fast as my little legs could run, almost in a cartoonish manner where it felt as if my feet were not touching the ground, just missing a nurse with a full tray of sectioned out meds, and yelled, "Come quick! Some asshole is hurting my brother!" Fortunately, Brett's doctor happened to be just down the hall at the nurse's station, so I grabbed him by the hand and we ran down the hall and into the inner room without a second of hesitation to pause for proper ICU sterile paper covering garb.

The intern was attempting another jab when, like lightening, the doctor grabbed the intern like a paper doll and forcibly tossed him aside yelling something like, "You have no idea what you are doing! You are unauthorized for this procedure! Who let you in here? You will never practice medicine at this hospital again! Now get out!" As the doctor calmed Brett, the inept intern scurried out the door, whimpering like the greasy sewer rat that he was. Brett's doctor finished the procedure with the ease of butter melting, and Brett did not feel a thing. We all took a collective deep breath. The energy shifted in the room.

The doctor looked at me when it was done, and in his eyes conveyed his understanding of the physical pain Brett suffered, as well as the emotional trauma we had both endured. For a moment, it seemed like time stood still and we were completely connected, our eyes meeting one another's as we gathered ourselves and took another deep breath. I remember looking into the doctor's eyes as if to say thank you, smiling under my now sweaty, soggy, and tear soaked face mask, hoping he'd see me smile, at least through my eyes, because I meant it deeply. He smiled back at me. I walked closer to Brett and tried to hug him tightly with my eyes because I thought if I actually touched him that may be too much for his little body to endure at the moment. I stroked his arm so softly I was not sure if I was actually touching him. I fought back my tears and tried to look brave for him. He smiled at me and for a slight moment, and what had been surreal and horrible, was now sweet and so deeply loving between just us. I wished that moment could have lasted for hours, but it was only a few seconds.

It seemed that the dust from that traumatic incident had barely settled when the time had come for Brett to be discharged. It had been a year since he was admitted. It was not a joyous release, but one that would at least get him out of that hospital. By this time, my 11-year old brother was so skinny that simple tasks like dressing himself was not entirely possible without some help from Mom and Dad. He could fit inside a standing foot locker with ease. He was very weak but would seem to manage a faint smile and still there remained a rascal-like twinkle in his eyes. I loved that! Leaving behind Shirley Temples, toxic cherries, bar buffets, jell-o, creepy bar dudes in bad brown corduroy, textured and saggy polyester, everything turquoise and even my Mom's purse-hidden chicken wings, we set off for home back to Oregon. My brother's medical team gave him a chance at recovery, but a very slim one. Regardless, at least that chance would take place in the comfort of our loud and crazy home, with our dog Max and cat Oreo, and donuts after church.

Crying Over Spilled Milk

Life as we knew it fumbled along at best. Dad returned to work, Mom made the frequent visits to the doctor's office with Brett, and my other brothers and I returned to our school classrooms. We tried our best to settle into as much of a normal life as possible. We went through our normal motions, but something was very different. People looked at us in a strange and different way. They hushed their voices when we'd see them, and sometimes they'd act overly-animated to compensate for their inability to sound casual. It was as if the local town clinic was offering free meds and everyone had taken advantage of it except for us.

I remember one night in particular only a couple of months after our return home when I couldn't sleep. I was tossing and turning, and it got to a point where I decided I'd go downstairs and get a glass of water and check on Brett. I crept down the hallway like a Ninja, then to the landing of our creaky stairs, in case Mom was in the kitchen and could hear me. I surveyed the area to make sure my late night wandering would not be noticed. The entire family was on edge and anything at all could set one of us off. As I got to the top of the steps, I could hear the hushed voices of my parents talking to Brett. I remember the uncomfortable knot in my stomach as I heard my brother crying, again asking, "why, why?" "Will I be able to go fishing and paint and eat chocolate cake wherever I'm going?" "What is heaven?" "Why can't I get better and stay here with you guys?" He had heard the type of news from my parents that a little kid should never have to hear, nor should any parent have to break such type of news to their child. And I heard it, too. My 7-year old self wanted to run down the stairs screaming, "No! Not my brother!" But I could barely breathe and my body failed to move at all from the stair from where I was perched.

I felt frightened and could only imagine what Brett must have been feeling! Again, time stood still. I remember crying too, and trying so hard to hold it inside as not to be detected by my parents or brother. My heart was pounding, my body was sweaty, my head was spinning, and it felt like I was going to vomit, all while the life was being choked out of me. It felt like I was being punched in the heart and stomach at the same time. I wanted to jump off the remaining five bottom stairs and go run and hug my brother, and tell him I love him and that he'd get better. I wanted to hug my parents and tell them it would all be ok. I needed a hug, too. But instead, my choking sobs gave me away and my parents got really upset. They yelled at me and sent me off to my room. I was crushed.

Earlier that day, Mom and Dad had received the final verbal punch from the doctor who'd given them the prognosis of leukemia five years prior. The cancer had now spread to Brett's internal organs and was aggressive. There was nothing more that could be done. My parents were given a choice to admit Brett back into a local hospital, where no real recovery was imminent, or to have their son live out his last months in the comfort of the family home. Brett was given less than a year to live, but time was not on his side. He didn't even make it past five months.

The next few weeks were bizarre. I felt like more of an alien in my own family and in my own skin. I'm sure that, looking back, my family members must have felt just as lost and scared as I did. There was little joy or laughter in the house. Even our pets seemed sad. My parents did their maximum best to handle everything, but the sadness, anger, uncertainty, confusion, and heaviness grew daily. We all walked around our house quiet, in pain, zombie like and trying our best to just hold it together.

There was one night in particular I remember all too well. While Dad was arriving home from work, Mom and I were cooking dinner. My two other brothers were off in their rooms doing something to allow them to hide and not have to prepare dinner or do any chores, those slackers. Mom asked me to bring Brett a cup of milk to try to coat his stomach and help alleviate his terrible nausea. By now, Brett permanently lived in the den on our fold out sofa bed couch, because he was not strong enough to climb the stairs to his bedroom. In fact, he could not even get out of bed by himself. The den was the place in the house where the family would gather together and either laugh, argue or cuss at the TV, and usually all of the above at the same time. The den was always our oasis of escaping the world. Now it had become a place in the house that felt condemned. We would visit with Brett and whether he liked it or not, we'd all converge upon him and argue over what programs to watch...every night. He tolerated us so patiently. I would look at him frequently thinking to myself but never asking him, if he wanted us there with him, if he wanted to talk, or if we annoyed the crap out of him. Brett would always just smile back at me as if reading my thoughts. It was his answer to everything. I loved that about him.

As I walked into the den that evening, I was aware that I approached him gently, cat-like. To be honest, since I was seven at the time, I couldn't begin to understand how he felt, or what must be going though emotionally, but I did know he was in constant and intense pain. I was a little scared of his illness, and of bringing him any further discomfort. I didn't even want to talk too loud because it looked like it hurt him just to listen. Well, there I was, and I was by his side to do my best to help him and Mom.

I had a cup of cold milk in my slightly shaking hands to give him and he looked over at me and smiled so completely and so gently as only he could right at me, as if to sense what I was feeling, in an attempt to comfort me. I knelt down beside him to try and help him drink the milk but I didn't fully comprehend what to do or how to help him be able to drink this milk with ease. I didn't know I had to lift his head up off his pillow to help him drink. I didn't know this was his condition. But I tried my best. As it turns out I didn't lift his head high enough as I tried to pour the milk into his delicate little mouth. I poured too fast. He got a little in his mouth but a lot of it spilled out the sides of his mouth, down his cheeks, and onto his neck and chest as he coughed from being choked by the very liquid that was there to help him. On the contrary, she looked at me with such disappointment at what I had just caused to happen, as if numb, I couldn't move. I didn't receive a hug. I ran upstairs confused, crying and took solace in my stuffed animals. As the shock of that incident began to sink in and as I lay on my bed sobbing into my teddy bears and headless Barbie dolls, I began to receive the weight of what my mom must have been trying to manage in that moment. My thoughts then shifted to my brother. How was it he could still smile at me after what I had done? Would he ever forgive me? I wanted to go hug him. I wanted to run away. I wanted a hug from Dad. I wanted to disappear.

So Lucky To Have The Flu

As to the exact number of days that passed between the 'crying over spilled milk' incident, and having to stay home from school because I was sick with the flu, I can't recall. We had as a family just celebrated

Brett's 12th birthday a couple weeks earlier. But now, there I was home sick, sitting on the floor in the den. It was early afternoon and I was wearing a long flannel nightgown, sitting on top of the heat vent, trying to trap all of the heat for myself with my night gown acting as a big tent. Yes, I was hogging the heat because I was trying to alleviate the intense chills I had. I was watching annoying daytime TV, and I remember thinking to myself, this is what my Grandma watches. What's wrong with me? Mom was in the fold out sofa bed couch sleeping next to my brother, which was just a few feet behind and to the left of where I was sitting, hogging the heat to myself.

Dad had just left about 30 minutes before, to go to his office to pick up more work, since he was primarily working from home these days, and to run some errands. I remember him saying he'd be back in about an hour. He bolted out the front door as if to rush in order to get back home faster. I knew he didn't want to be away from his eldest son even for a few minutes. My youngest brother was at a friend's house nearby on a play date, and my second oldest brother was in school just down the street a few blocks away. Mom was peacefully snoring in bed next to my brother and all seemed to be in it's place.

That's when I heard something. Something was not right. The energy in the room shifted and felt very strange, thick. It was my brother. From what I could hear over the TV., and from the noises coming from him, it seemed like he was trying to get comfortable, shifting around a bit. I thought I heard murmuring of voices or his voice. Who was he talking to? It is slightly foggy as to the precise noises I heard, but undeniably I heard voices over the sappy daytime tv drama. But it was odd because I knew he couldn't really move at all on his own anymore and he was too weak to even roll over onto his side or lift his head by himself, yet clearly he was shifting about. When I looked over my left shoulder at him, he was sitting up in bed with such an exquisite smile on his face, as if being propped up magically. He looked as though he were glowing. Something in me was trying to wake me up to really see what was occurring in front of my eyes, but at the same time it felt like I was swimming through wet oatmeal. I felt suddenly very heavy and could neither move nor speak. I wanted to jump up and go to him, but at the same time I felt lethargic and numb, my body failing to respond in real time. I felt a bolt of energy run through me, but still I sat motionless, while my mind played a maniacal game of pinball. What was wrong with me?! All I could do was manage to smile back at him. The room felt suddenly crowded. It was a moment in time that seemed to hang on, as we smiled at each other, in full yet wordless communication. It was pin drop silence. It was a silence that I was destined to revisit. That moment is burned into my consciousness to this day.

I finally found my voice, as if something had released my mind meld, and asked him, "Do you need anything?" "Are you alright?" Smiling still, he replied, "No, I'm just really tired." I replied, "You should lay down then and get some sleep." His response seemed to be one of immense relief as if it were the sweetest victory, I guess if you could qualify it as such. He replied, ..."Yes...", with a sigh-like quality to his breath. For some odd reason, I took my eyes off of him and looked back at the crappy daytime TV show that I was not at all interested in. Why did I do that? Why didn't I go over to him? It was as if my head was meant to be turned away for what was happening next. I felt like a puppet with no control over myself or my thoughts. In what felt to be a few seconds later, after he had laid back down, I began to hear strange gasps and labored breathing coming from my brother. It was as though he was breathing and choking at the same time. The numbness I had just felt in my body had instantly turned into a shock! I knew now in the pit of my stomach what was happening. As my head flung around again to look at Brett, my breathing soared into an anaerobic state in a second. I wanted to run over to his side but it was too late. There was one last long labored breath in. And one last long exhale that seemed to last longer than humanly possible. And that was it. He was gone.

As if a surge of electricity forcibly entered my puppet body, I felt a new strength in me and called out, "What's wrong?" "Brett, are you ok?" "Do you need some help?" As one eye closes, another one opens. Mom heard me talking and certainly heard the panic in my voice as I said to her, "Mom, wake up!" "Something is wrong with Brett!" "I can't hear him breathing!"

As divine grace would have it, Brett passed literally seconds before Mom awoke. When she came to, she went into her E.R. Nurse mode trying to revive him using mouth-to-mouth and CPR, but nothing worked. Thank God his struggle was over. He lay lifeless and non-reactive to Mom's panicked attempts to bring him back. As I stood over them, I felt such a bizarre combination of sadness for my Mom, yet enveloped in such joy and relief for Brett. It was as if he crossed the finish line to the life he came here to live, knowing that he had done what he had come to do with full victory. Everything sped up from there. Mom was sobbing, I was sobbing, we were trying to manage as best we could, but it was sheer chaos. It was a cocktail of confusion, panic, disbelief, shock, grief and fear that Mom and I were force fed. She told me to follow her into the kitchen to help her call dad, call the school, the neighbors, the priest, and the funeral home to bring the hearse. Those were the days of rotary dial phones and phone books. Our normal, usual phone in that moment, had become something of a torture device. Not to mention it was baby shit green and the dial wheel was cracked after suffering a rather violent hang up from one of us.

The phone didn't seem to be able to dial at the warp speed Mom's fingers were intending. She was fumbling through the phone book and I was trying to help look up the numbers but I couldn't do any right by her no matter how hard I tried. It also didn't help that I was shaking and sweating as I fumbled over the phonebook to find the right numbers for her to dial. Finally she yelled at me to go back into the den and close my brother's eyes. I was mortified. Holy shit! What?! Really?! Me? All by myself? But I was caught between not doing what Mom told me to do, and terrified at angering her, so I walked slowly down the hallway, back into the den where now a strange and eery smell and energy began to enter the room. I walked up to my brother's body, outstretched my hand to do the duty Mom told me to do, but I just couldn't do it! I asked his forgiveness. Mom rushed into the room and said, "Never mind, I'll do it!" "Go get his toothbrush and brush his teeth." Holy shit! What?! Really? Me? I failed again at this task and was sent up to my room. It was a madhouse. My head was spinning and I threw up all over my flannel nightgown.

There was not the moment of peace I had envisioned with Brett floating up through the house on his way up to Heaven. Surely he'd seen me bumbling and he might be mad at me, too. I flew back down those stairs so fast I had no feeling of them underneath my feet. I went back into the den to his bedside and knelt down and completely lost it. Sobbing, scared and yet strangely relieved for him. He left this life with such love, humor, grace, acceptance and peace. It was a timeless moment I had experienced with him, and one that left a profound imprint.

By this time, maybe 30 minutes had passed since Brett had died and layers upon layers of anger, yelling, crying and murmured conversation overlapped one another from strange people who started floating in and out of our house, numbly milling around. This disturbance seemed to go on for hours, and then days. The priest had arrived to give Brett's body the final prayers, Dad came home to see the hearse parked in front of our home. I will never forget the look on his face. He was beside himself with grief and anger. My brothers drifted in the front door one by one, with such a look of fear and confusion, it was as if they felt they were in the wrong house. A few other people peeked their heads around corners of the main floor nearby the den. Who were all of these people? I seemed to not recognize anyone except my family members, Brett's pediatrician, and Brett's lifeless body. As I knelt down by the side of my brother's body, I noticed I was almost completely wet with tears. I looked at the crucifix on the wall just over my left shoulder as if wanting to communicate with it the harder I stared at it. I noticed through all of the commotion, chaos and hushed voices that

I physically felt better. I felt no more nausea, no more chills, no more sore throat. This got my attention.

> *"When we have the ability to receive the silence in our heart, then automatically the purification of the silence gives a part of the highest information."*

-Sri Kaleshwar

Earth Element Exercises

Silent Meditation

If possible, meditate outdoors while sitting on the ground. Before you get comfortable for your Earth Element Meditation, stand barefoot and with eyes closed, take five deep breaths. Connect deeply to Mother Earth as you visualize your body as a vessel or like a drinking straw. Try to "see" the energy you choose to release in this meditation leave out through your feet, and "see" the brightest white/silver light enter in through the top of your head. This brilliant, Divine energy is all around you. And now you are bringing your focus to drawing into your body this energy to create both a deep purification and a powerful flooding in of new, positive vibrations.

Once you feel the connections, begin your seated Earth Element Meditation by placing a blanket or towel underneath your body to create a small barrier between you and the earth. If you need to sit in a chair for any reason, place a small towel or blanket underneath your feet. Create the intention that you are summoning the heart of Mother Earth and you are meditating to Her with your intentions. Who better than Mother Divine to know what's in your heart? Whatever you have been through in your life that has caused an earthquake or two, She is there for you. Call upon Her and know that you are absolutely connected to Her because you are an aspect of Her. Create a strong bond with Mother Earth, speak internally to Her, then sit in silence and see what comes to you.

When you feel complete, open your eyes and reconnect with your body. Reach for your *Soul Journal* and write down anything and everything that came as a result of your meditation. Sometimes an image comes, sometimes numbers, sometimes a message, and even a reflection from Nature in a gust of wind, a surge of inspiration, or from a bird or animal in nature making a sound or sudden movement. Have no expectations and no agenda from your meditation. Sometimes the messages or reflections from nature come hours or days later. Be patient and know that from your intention and attention in meditation, Mother will answer you. Have faith. It is always your heartwaves that connect you deepest to The Divine.

You are welcome to repeat your Earth Element Meditation for as many days in a row as you feel you need in order to reach a feeling of self assurance or completion of the Earth Element. Do not rush into the next chapter until you feel ready, but at the same time, stay on track with your *Soul Journey Process*, picking up the Fire Element next.

Soul Journaling Exercise

1. Prepare your Sacred Space by lighting your candle(s), incense, and by getting comfortable and cozy. Adjust the lighting so that only the candles are providing light and there are no competing electrical vibrations.
2. Put on any beautiful and melodious music to help create peaceful and loving vibrations.
3. Take five deep breaths and release completely. Breathe either through your nose or through your mouth, whichever is most comfortable and relaxing for you.
4. Sit with your eyes closed for a moment to allow yourself to observe how you feel by what this chapter brought up for you. Compassionately keep in mind that every *personal*

earthquake brings Divine opportunity for incredible change. Remember that even in nature, we see that through natural disaster comes the birth of fresh life and pure positive potential.

5. What is the lesson in the experience(s)? Where can you apply *forgiveness* to yourself and to others who were a part of your experience? Where can you find *humor* in your experience? Where can you apply *love*?

"In the universe, the most beautiful is Her (Divine Mother).
Her nature, the Creation, is both positive and negative.
Without the shadow you cannot recognize the light."

-Sri Kaleshwar

Chapter Two

Fire Element

"God is equal to peace, Peace is equal to God. God is equal to Silence, Silence is equal to God."

-Sri Kaleshwar

Testing, Testing...1, 2, 3

The odor in the room began to shift as people drifted out one by one, and as I remained kneeling by the side of the tired fold out sofa couch which still held my brother's lifeless body, a massive floodgate opened. Sudden and new questions flew from somewhere into my mind, bubbling up with so many questions about what had actually just happened. And as these questions flew out of me, I looked over my left shoulder again to the crucifix on our wall and felt consumed by confusion, sadness and anger. Where were the band of Angels that are supposed to appear at the time of death? Wasn't God actually supposed to appear? How did I miss Him?

Strong feelings of conviction and determination began coursing through me and almost instantaneously I became fixed on needing to find out what happened. Of course to the naked eye, my brother had died. But what REALLY happened? Where did the life that was just in my brother go? Did that life force have a name? What is death? What is life? How come I couldn't see the life in my brother leave? But how come I could feel it? What had happened to him in those moments just before he passed that he was able to sit up so effortlessly and look literally as if he were glowing? Where was Jesus now when I needed him most? Where was the voice of God that I had heard talked about so much in church when I needed to hear it? Why didn't anyone seem to know what the hell was going on? Why did my brother get sick and not someone else? If prayers really worked, why didn't all the prayers for my brother to get well seem completely ineffective? I felt robbed and cheated and I was pissed.

Experiencing such an earthquake that day ignited such a fire in me, I became determined to get some answers. I had no idea what the journey would entail but I was ready. I was in this for the long haul, but secretly hoped I didn't have to wait too long. I would have no way of knowing my search would take many years, and would push me to such extremes.

A Long, Hot, Confusing Wandering in the Desert

The years following my brother's passing, from 1976-1999, I was between the ages of 8 and 32. These years were a test to say the least. The family dynamic was strained and strange, and for good reason. Life felt void of positive function and there was this huge hole in each one of us like a sinkhole in our hearts. We'd manage smiles and normal, routine behavior to daily life, like my brothers and I making obscene gestures at each other, or telling them I had a "big boobie lady" sighting at the grocery store, but to me, I felt even more out of place and alone than ever before.

My parent's marriage became more tense and strained as the years passed, eventually resulting in a brief separation then divorce. They attempted to hold it together for us kids but it just never recovered. Because they never recovered. No one recovered. Dad consumed himself in his work and Mom became more removed and isolated, unable to find balance or solace. Without the ability to process our emotions, there were almost constant arguments and outbursts. Our dog Max even developed a curious case of Bells Palsey from the high levels of stress in the house. The more they yelled and fought, the more it made us want to run and hide, so although not a fan of school at all except for art, recess and after school sports, I actually liked going because it got me away from the madness. Mom was being presented like never before with such a darkness inside of her, so she slept more, was less active, smoked a lot and was just overall a shell of a human being. She tried to stay involved as best she could. She'd take us to school events, to the orthodontist, and she'd even come to my track meets after school. Granted, she'd show up in her nightgown with a parka covering her, wearing socks and flip flops, smoking a cigarette, cheering me on as I sprinted down the track competing in the 100 meter, long jump and short relay. In hindsight, I give her credit for pulling it together enough to remember I had a track meet and for showing up in style. Her fashion sense never quite caught on though. God bless her.

Bruce, now almost 10, had taken the open role as the oldest, although reluctantly. He started going off on his own, withdrawing from the family. This left me and 5-year old Bart to one another's care. There were times when my brothers and I would hang out together, playing wiffle ball, tag, and when it was fund raising time for Boy Scouts, we'd go door to door gathering collections like a suburban street gang. I volunteered to make the collection rounds with them but not because I loved them that much, or even that I cared at all about the Boy Scouts; candy was my sole incentive, and it was given freely by our nicer neighbors. I recall one time, just after Mom had given me a "boy's haircut" when I tagged along with my brothers for an afternoon of collection rounds. I was feeling quite gawky and bald, so I put one of those fake flowers glued to a hair pin in my hair to draw attention to the fact I was, in fact, still a girl. I made the fake flower so prominent it was practically right above my forehead to make it blatantly obvious. I found pleasure in teasing my brothers as they were dressed in their ugly uniform garb as we all walked up the steps to the front door of this one house and when the old man answered the door, he said, "well hello boys, how are you today?" Boys?! With all shyness aside, I blurt out with my lisp,

"Hey, can't you see? I'm a guur you Fucko!" My brothers started laughing which made me run away, which made them run away. I think they had to hit up Dad for the money owed by that one old man because they never went back to collect. And my favorite light blue glued on flower hairpin was lost that day from my sprint home, candy clutched tightly in my fists. I think it was not long after that that I was kicked out of Brownies for flipping off the Head Brownie Lady. I was on a roll and the shit show had just begun.

My schoolwork seemed meaningless and I was uninspired. I remember getting teased a lot since I could not pronounce my "Rs", and that was a curse for a girl by the name of Marcie Regina Anderson, who was a bit on the shy side to begin with. When my teachers would call on me to answer in the classroom, questions that seemed unimportant, I would hear snickering and then laughter, which made me begin to stutter a bit. I am quite sure I gave a few of the kids the middle finger from behind my back more than once. It didn't take me long before I quickly chose to clam up and not raise my hand anymore, nor answer my teachers when they would call on me in order to avoid the inevitable taunting and teasing from the other kids. Not long after a few of these incidents, I was put into the "special kids" reading group because my teachers thought something was wrong with me. I chose to instead be sent to the principal's office as punishment for my silence. It seemed odd to me, being sent to the principal's office for reacting to being teased. At least that's how I saw things. But it was the 70s and there were bad choices being made left and right; the horrendous fashions, inhaling of toxic fumes from massive layers of Aqua Net on our bad hair, inappropriately large eye glasses, tinfoil blue eye shadow, smoking cigarettes, and copious amounts of plaid amongst bubbled, lumpy polyester. Mom and Dad didn't go to bat for me, but to their defense, I never told them, and they likely never heard about it from the principal's office. And really, we were all just trying to get through.

Survival Was Our Coping Mechanism

Family dinner time was a time to gather together, to share our day with each other, maybe crack a few jokes, which I liked. The family dog would turn on his charm and inch closer and closer to the dinner table, like a skilled Navy Seal approaching his target, putting one paw over the line of kitchen floor to dining room carpet, then he'd look away as not to make eye contact with Dad. I loved his slyness. We were kindred spirits for sure. Someone would inevitably spill something, someone would fart, burp, laugh, fall down, or cry. Every night. But now it carried such a heavy weight and the conversation was typically awkward at best, or maybe that's just how I felt. I can't remember one of my teachers or counselors sitting with me to ask me how I was coping to the new 'adjustments' in my family. I guess things like that were just not done back then. Again, it seemed so strange to me that nobody was talking at all about the many facets of what had happened. People seemed like robots to me so I chose to channel my anger, frustration and hurt through writing, sketching, comedy and sports.

A fire began to build inside me. I wanted solid answers to my myriad of questions. I wanted someone to listen to me, to help me to understand my pain, my fears, my confusion, my anger, my dreams and my sadness. I needed someone to hug me and look me in the eyes and say, "Yes, I can help you understand, and once you understand more, you will heal from this and feel better." But instead, it felt hopeless, as if I was screaming my very hardest, calling out for this magic person with the Truth to appear, but into a whirling tornado in the middle of nowhere.

My search for God began by about 9-years old. I remember calling private meetings with nuns and priests, imagining myself to be a badass investigative reporter. I would arrive, pencil and paper in hand, to get some God-answers out of them. But each time I asked the questions, the same bizarre replies came. "I don't know my child." What?! "Why do you want to know where the soul goes after death?" With the heads tilted of to one side saying, "I can't explain what the soul is." "I don't know why it was your brother who got sick and not another child." "Try harder in school, say 10 Hail Marys, be obedient to your parents and be a good girl." "Pray and be at peace." Between the cussing out of them at one extreme and the loud crickets to the other extreme, I threw my hands up. I condemn them all.

Yes, it's true, I put good use to my truck driver mouth. You can only imagine the verbal symphony, gathered from years of pain and confusion which came flying out in protest to their lame answers. I had heard these same answers to my questions for months upon months now and I had heard just about enough! The nonverbal cussing wasn't cutting it anymore. I stood up to one priest after our brief meeting and said with conviction, "Well, if you don't know what the hell's going on, why are you a damn priest?" I like to imagine I was the cause for a few priests to change careers. God bless them.

If You Mentally Flip Someone Off, Does Anyone Hear a Tree Fall in the Forest?

I got kicked out of CCD, an after school church study session, for mentally flipping off a nun. I think she heard it. She must have seen it in the reflection of my eyes. I challenged her non-answers and this was not ok. It was fine with me, but apparently not her. For a few weeks until my parents figured out what had really happened, I was dropped off at CCD, but then made my way with a skip in my step to the local 7-11 for my cherry cola Slurpie fix, then back just in time for my parents to pick me up. I was tired of being put off to the side and silenced as if that were going to magically help the answers to my questions appear. Maybe they thought I'd weaken and give up my search. Nope. Not at all. On the outside I was a scrawny little girl with slightly buck teeth and resembling a fumbling colt, but on the inside I was a molten volcano ready to crucify anyone who gave me the wrong answers or tried to stop me from finding out the Truth.

I felt helpless, frustrated, confused and mislead. I felt alien. The ones who were supposed to help me on the path to find the God-connection were just as lost as I was. This began to frighten me. I cried bullshit on the whole thing and quit going to church all together. I recall a particular line to a prayer in the mass we'd recite out loud. I hated saying it because I didn't believe it was true. In fact I would not say it. It was before taking holy communion (the bread/body of Christ and wine/blood of Christ part), but before we could partake and be cleansed of our sins, we had to recite out loud, "Lord, I am not worthy to receive you...." Oh yes I am, and I'll prove it, God damn it! Now get out of my way. It's donut time. Amen.

My anger and fiery side came to work to my advantage as I fueled it into athletics, humor and eventually, my work. It didn't play out too well with the boyfriends I had though...

Dad used to describe me to others as 'a flea on a hot rock'. Subtle. At the time, it was clear he and I had been cut from the same cloth of impatience. We wore it well. We flew our flag. I played fast pitch softball, and had such speed around the bases and a great arm as a leftie, I got put in at catcher, first base, center field, right field, shortstop and third base. Not all at once. I played basketball and was a nightmare to anyone I played defense against. It was offense I was not so smooth nor consistent at. Basketball was not my jam. I played volleyball and was a fairly strong server and outside hitter. And yes, team comic and champion braider of hair.

Once I was in my late teens, I entered into fashion runway modeling and athletic/sports modeling, working for the top companies out of Portland and Seattle. Humor was always my spice of choice and used it often. I enjoyed making others laugh. I used humor on the runway when the model is supposed to be seen and not heard. Not me. I was heard. I went to college in Portland but walked away from it after about a year and a half. I wanted to try my hand at the corporate world, and frankly was impatient with all of the school stuff. I was hired by a local ad agency and did very well, but after about four years walked away from it and became a certified personal trainer. Finally! This was a blend of the elements of both work and pleasure that clicked for me. It felt like I was at home in this work. I could keep up my own fitness regime while working and was paid well for it. As I began to work with private clients, I could spend more time outdoors, in nature and make my own hours. And as my private client base expanded into all socio-economic and varied demographic backgrounds, I noticed rather quickly that no matter what we do, where we came from in life, or what our present situation, a common thread between us all is some level of suffering and heartbreak. My clients would open up to me about deep issues, deep pains and unmet desires, and I noticed I truly wanted to help relive their suffering and be able to provide them with the truthful answers they needed. The very same answers I needed. But who was I fooling? The sting of all of those unanswered questions and any actual deeper feeling of connection to The Divine for myself was missing. My internal search and struggle continued.

Life was going along well and I quickly became booked with coveted modeling jobs, balancing out my time between gigs training private clients. I loved the freedom of being able to train with them in the gym, their homes, or outdoors, helping them to lose weight, gain strength, definition, and tone, improve flexibility and guiding them to become more confident, balanced and happy. I really loved helping others. I felt confident in my work and in my innate ability to help others beyond surface level. I was making good money, I had good friends, and I had a sense of purpose that fed me. I enjoyed it. Seemingly I had the world by the short hairs. I felt layers of hurt and anger begin to drift away. The more my clients shared with me about their lives and what they were seeking real help with, beyond the weight loss, wanting to be more desirable to their partner, or gaining improved flexibility, was relief from suffering, a lack of feeling worthy and confident, and heartbreak on any level. All levels. They desired real relief. No bandaid. Complete healing.

They wanted to know there was something out there, something real. They wanted to feel a profound and undeniable connection to the Divine. And I could hear a voice in my head shout out, "Me too!" "I want to experience that!" They wanted to know complete healing was even possible. So did I! Though I didn't know how, I knew all of this and more was possible. Feeling truly loved and being loved is our birthright. But where was this information and these healing techniques, and where was the person that could teach me? How many grueling years was my search going to take? My flame was becoming a tiny flicker yet would not go out. It couldn't go out. I protected it tirelessly.

Something deep down began to stir in me, to my very core. There was a faint voice that seemed to rise up inside of me almost as if it were climbing out of a darkened, dank well. It's strength grew and it disturbed me. And as it approached closer, it became stronger, it frightened me. That voice was a part of me, a part of me I had stuffed down by my own distracted thoughts and limited beliefs. I had nearly given up on that voice. *But it had not given up on me.* That part of me returned and reminded me it still wanted those answers I sought as a child when I knelt at the side of my brother's lifeless body. I needed the answers as badly as I needed to breathe, to eat, and to stay alive. I was nearing the threshold of a time for a huge change in my life, and although apprehensive, I felt curious, fearless, exhilarated. I craved the profound, even dared it to find me. I craved my own experiences of the unexpected. I had no way of knowing that an incredible shift so penetrating existed for me, let alone was right around the corner.

The Fire of Desire

It mattered to me in the most sincere way that I was able to help my clients heal from their heartbreak, sadness, feelings of unworthiness, high levels of stress, fear, addiction and anxiety. Was it too much to ask that my clients lead a happy, peaceful, satisfied and love-filled life? And hey, what about me, too? But how? And who was I kidding? How could I truly help them when I knew very clearly, that I felt heartbroken myself. I had frustration, anger, and sadness that I could not totally heal over the years, no matter how much I ran, worked out or cracked myself up with my comedy and antics. So far nothing truly had helped me to heal. So now what? There began this powerful friction inside of me, knocking at me with such impact, it felt like this force was gaining and it was like trying to rub two sticks together to make a fire, but those sticks were me! Nothing mattered more than having this desire met.

My career in modeling and in private training was now in full swing. In looking back, it all seemed quite natural and easy for me and I felt blessed to have such a full and glamorous life. I had always been a hard worker, disciplined, loyal and responsible. I genuinely liked people and being around an energy of personal growth, physical health and possibility. But the truth was, something was missing. I was working hard, but was restless. I was sought after, but unhappy. I was praised, but it didn't seem to matter. I felt like an imposter. What was wrong with me? What was I really here to do in this lifetime? My inner conflict was relentless. I realized I had ever been at peace in my entire life. This epiphany hit hard and made me cry…a lot. I knew much more was out there for me to experience. Now, I just needed to find what could take me to the next place in my search. There began an internal wrestling match. Change was brewing.

In 1996 at the age of 29, I was given a chance to move to Los Angeles where a larger modeling and commercial agency wanted to sign me. That is exciting stuff right? Holy crap! For me, it was all a blur. All I knew was that it meant getting out of Oregon and into a larger market with greater and new possibilities. I felt special. But not in an entitled way, and I got over it fast. Now was my chance to expand my personal training career, my modeling career and to begin to look into what it meant to become a healer. *This was exciting.* This was the opportunity to change my life, and change it sure did, beyond my capacity to comprehend at the time.

> *"Every person's progress depends on the way of his thoughts; deep silence thoughts, peaceful thoughts. Not getting confusion. Sitting relaxedly, getting thoughts on whatever thing you're going to do.*
>
> *Then once more thinking, once more thinking. Then 100% victory is waiting."*

-Sri Kaleshwar

Fire Element Exercises

Silent Meditation

1. Prepare your Sacred Space by lighting your candle(s), incense, and by getting comfortable and cozy. Adjust the lighting so that only the candles are providing light and there are no competing electrical vibrations. For this particular meditation, you will need to stare at a candle for as long as you are able without blinking. Naturally after a few minutes your eyes will sting and a tear or two will form, but still hold out as long as you can before you blink. This is a deep purification of your eyes through the candle flame. After you do blink a bit, return to your open eyed connection to the candle flame.

2. Put on any beautiful and melodious music to help create peaceful and loving vibrations.

3. Take five deep breaths and release completely. Breathe either through your nose or through your mouth, whichever is most comfortable and relaxing for you.

4. Sit with your eyes closed for a moment to allow yourself to observe how you feel by what this chapter brought up for you. Compassionately keep in mind that with every *burning desire* brings divine opportunity for incredible change. Even in nature we can see that through *natural disaster comes the birth of fresh life and pure potential for a new start.*

5. What is the lesson in the experience(s)? Where can you apply *forgiveness* to yourself and to others who were a part of your experience? Where can you find *humor* in your experience? Where can you apply *love*?

Soul Journaling Exercise

Meditate comfortably inside while sitting on the ground or comfortable chair. As mentioned earlier, place a new candle on your meditation table or altar and light it. Connect deeply to the flame and visualize your body as a vessel or straw and as you *see* the energy you choose to release in this meditation leave out your eyes, *see* the brightest white/silver light enter in through the top of your head to fill your body. This brilliant, divine energy is all around you. And now, doing your best not to blink your eyes for as long as possible, you are bringing your focus to accessing or drawing into you this energy to create both a deep purification and a powerful flooding in of new, positive vibrations. You may feel quite drowsy after this process, so please allow yourself to rest your eyes or even sleep for a bit when you are finished.

When you are ready, begin your Fire Element Meditation by creating the intention of summoning the energy of the sun, as seen in the candle flame. You are meditating your intentions to the sun. In the Indian tradition, it is believed that the sun is one part a Creator. Relate directly this power of the sun's energy into your body and your intentions of *burning* and letting go of negative emotions. Allow as a balance, the powerful healing energy of the sun/fire to support the healing effects of the negative emotions or patterning, much like how the sun's heat helps everything grow by giving it's warmth. Whatever it is that has caused destructive emotions, it is time to let it all go. Call upon Mother Divine and know that you are absolutely connected to Her because you are an aspect of Her, and all Five Elements are in you. Create a strong bond with Mother Divine, speak internally to Her, then sit in silence and see what comes to you.

Once you are ready, reach for your *Soul Journal* and write down anything and everything that came as a result of your meditation. Sometimes an image comes, sometimes numbers, sometimes a message, and even a reflection from nature in a phone call from someone you have not heard from in a long time, a surge of inspiration, or from a thought that has magically popped into your head that is the exact answer or direction you were seeking. Have no expectations and no agenda from your meditation. Sometimes the messages or reflections from nature come hours or days later. Be patient and know that from your intention and attention in meditation, Mother will answer you. *Have faith.*

You are welcome to repeat your Fire Element Meditation for as many days in a row as you feel you need in order to reach a feeling of self assurance or completion of the Fire Element. Do not rush into the next chapter until you feel ready, but at the same time, stay on track with your *Soul Journey Process*, picking up the Sky Element next.

> *"To any problem there is a solution to that. Even though there's a terrible darkness, through the Divine knowledge you can remove it."*
>
> -Sri Kaleshwar

Chapter Three

Sky Element

"Dharma is growing when we have a forgiving nature, showing mercy and kindness. You have no idea how much is hidden in the kindness."

-Sri Kaleshwar

A Road Not At All Well Traveled

Early one morning, packed tightly into my little Nissan Sentra with a strong cup of coffee and my possessions blocking my comfort, visibility, and almost sheer ability to drive, I set out from Portland to Los Angeles, stopping in Modesto for a brief visit with Grandma. I knew she would feed me well, and I would get more than my fill of home baked chocolate chip cookies. No argument there. I would enjoy a nice visit and I would get a lot of sleep. Grandma was an amazing cook. She was Betty Crocker on steroids. In fact, grandma had an inherent Master Chef quality to her that made Betty Crocker eligible only for a pimped out lemonade stand. She was humble and a hard worker. She had only one child, a son. Dad. I enjoyed my visit with her and we shared a few laughs at dad's expense. What else was there for us to laugh about over our cookies and coffee? We giggled and laughed as we verbally roasted her son into the wee hours of the night, which meant we were both in bed by 10:30.

Back on the road, well-rested and sugared up, I felt a sense of excitement and confidence at my exciting undertaking and a new life ahead. I took full advantage of being in my car alone channel surfing the radio, singing with no care for pitch, tone or volume, owning every song I sang. Barry Manilow to Helen Reddy, The Bee Gees to Hall and Oates, with a lot of tire commercials sprinkled in between music sets. Long road trip music play lists are a crap shoot. I felt pretty lucky with my options. I knew deep down I was distracting myself, trying to direct my chocolate chip cookie high to help drown out the fear that began to mentally box with me, and it was a buzz kill to my jam with John Denver. What the hell was I doing moving all the way to Los Angeles without a stable job, no real friends to lean on, and barely enough money to live for three months at best? I felt possessed. I drove on.

I arrived in Los Angeles after reaching as far as I possibly could before driving into the ocean. I had my wits about me and knew that would actually have been too far. I pulled into a gas station in Santa Monica to make a call. It was a payphone. Gross. I probably should have gone straight to a clinic to get a Hepatitis shot after using it, but time was of the essence. I had no map with me, no Tomas Guide, and no cell phone, not to mention, I had no idea where I was even going to live. I did have a definite-maybe lined up in Manhattan Beach but in looking back, I was signing up for complete and utter disturbance and insanity in my life. That order came through with flying colors. But no matter. I had a positive attitude, like Mary Tyler Moore when she flings her beret into the air smiling at the possibilities of her new life, and I was ready to take on whatever what was to come. But I had no beret.

I Clicked My Heels and Wound Up in Hell

I settled temporarily in Manhattan Beach and made contact with my new agency. I found a neighborhood gym where I could meet the locals and gain new private training clients. I was hopeful. This little gym was better suited for me in comparison to the one in West Hollywood where my greeting was getting frontally grabbed as a 'hello, this is my territory' by the gym manager, a woman by the way. I would have preferred a business card exchange, or even a slight smile, but that was not in my hands. I apparently was in her hands, but not for long before I excused myself to the door almost in full sprint and into my car. My interest in seeking out local wellness centers for training and classes in the Healing Arts was on the side, but it was still there, a curiosity and reality that would soon take over every aspect of my life as I knew it. After my studies in India, I learned it is always the soul that is in charge and it is the soul that is here for the body. It is not the body that is that important. The body is only a vehicle for the soul. Of course it is important to take good care of your body, but you get my point.

I had not been in Los Angeles for more than about 2 1/2 months when I had a final call-back audition for a well-known International sportswear/shoe company. I was psyched! It was my chance at a national tv commercial and it just felt like it was supposed to be my welcome gift to Los Angeles. It was the big break I was searching for, and I was ready to receive it.

Mentally creating the scene in the Disney film Cinderella, where she awakened to the birds singing and fluttering around her as she primped and danced, I showed up a little early and prepared for the audition. I quickly got the vibe from the somber cavemen on the field to tone down my joy a bit, one conveyed by his pointed finger and grunts. I remember signing in, being greeted by the casting agency, photographer and assistants, and being asked to help adjust the hurdles with a couple other models who had also arrived a little early, but clearly not as joyfully as I. Don't get me wrong, I had already stretched and jogged a few laps of the inner baseball diamond area. *I was good.* But it seemed a bit odd to be asked to help this 'professional' crew to arrange the hurdles, but hey, I am a helper, so I was on the job without hesitation. However, I soon found out none of them had a flipping clue what a hurdle even was. An uneasiness began to percolate from my gut.

I walked out onto the field and lent a helping hand. This is about when it really hit me. I was helping set up hurdles on the low cut grass in the outfield of a baseball field in Los Angeles. Not on a smooth surfaced track. Why weren't we on a real track? By nature, hurdles were not my thing, remembering I think I pulled a Pete Rose over the hurdles in High School, but I was certainly confident and athletic enough and could pass for looking like I knew what I was doing. It is how you look, not what you can do, right? No. Not at all, it turns out.

A nervousness began to consume me and I began to get an uncomfortable queasiness in my stomach. Clearly these hurdles were not spaced perfectly and by looking at the physicality of the director and his PA crew, I don't think they had been within 25 miles of a gym recently, let alone they had not hurdled a day in their lives— hurled perhaps more than a few times in back alley garbage cans, after too many beer bong doses, but hurdled? I began to pace a little and felt cagey. In that moment, metaphorically I felt the Angel on one shoulder and the Devil on the other, with the Angel begging me not to jump, but the Devil playing into my fears and ego, and convincing me I needed to do this. Damn Devil!

My shyness and inability to speak up for myself at the time drowned out my pounding heart and fear. As soon as I heard my name being called, I took off like a deer startled out of the woods by the sound of a hunter's bullet. I blindly proceeded to fly over the first hurdle. I came off of it fine but the next one was at a slightly shorter distance from the first and I came off a little off balance. I could feel the fear inside of me screaming at me to pull off and stop the audition! But that did not happen. I tried to correct my mis-stride after coming off the second hurdle but I could not correct enough and came off the last and final hurdle more off balance and at a faster pace than before. *Crash.* I landed in a slight divot with my right foot from a full speed pace, which caused a chain reaction of my entire body. I was like a human slinky but not in a good way. Kind of like in the way the actual slinky does work, as opposed to how the commercials make it look like it works. Which is not really at all. My right knee bent all the way out from the inside to the left and my body came crashing down hard onto the ground in the opposite direction. My *entire* body. It felt like my knee snapped in half in the direction the knee does not naturally bend, nor should ever bend. It was like being a doll in the hands of an evil giant, and my right knee was being used as his dental floss.

The world had stopped. It felt like my heart stopped. I felt time stood still. I hadn't had that shock of an experience since my brother's death. A panicked hush fell over the entire audition as it came to a screeching halt. I lay on the ground writhing in pain, clutching my right knee, and trying my damnedest not to cry, or vomit or both. That lasted only a few seconds and the tears sprang from my eyes uncontrollably. Nobody came over to help me for what seemed to be 5 minutes. Like a pack of hyenas watching their stricken prey, slowly a few models and a few others came over to check on me, circling and whispering and a few laughing. "Are you ok?" "What's wrong with her?" "Dude…did you see that?" "Can you get up?" "Is the knee supposed to bend that way?" "Good thing she didn't land in some dog crap." "She's not very good at the hurdles." "She's blonde, of course she can't hurdle." Already my knee had ballooned up to the size of a cantaloupe and was throbbing intensely. *This was bad.* I needed some serious medical help and fast. After what seemed to be 10 minutes, the director in charge of this audition approached me with what looked like to be a mustard stained collared shirt and with a tone of utter annoyance and asked, "Could you move off the field, we're trying to finish up this audition on time, and my ass is on the line if I screw up." Charming fella. I was shocked but lifted my head off the dirt to look at him, I grit my teeth at the searing pain, and asked, "Could you please call me an ambulance or can I use your cell phone?" He just looked at me void of emotion and said, "Yeah, you can use my cell but make it quick. I'm expecting a call", as he scratched himself frontally. He then tossed it at me. Good thing I had good hands to catch or I would have been pelted in the head by his phone. Sweet guy. A real catch. I was mortified!

I would have called him the F-word but I didn't have the strength. So I did mentally. *Twice.* Was this how people really treated each other? Where in the hell was I?! Was I actually in hell? Did I take a wrong turn off of the 10? Nobody lent me a hand to help me get up. Nobody! Who were these people and what was going on? I literally crawled a bit until I could manage standing and hopping on one leg, but with each hop, my now broken knee screamed out in further pain.

I had called the ambulance and by now one of the P.A.'s came over to help me to a nearby bench with about ten hops to go, so I could get off the field, off the ground and get my leg somewhat elevated. Being comfortable was out of the question, but at least out of the way had become possible. By now I had at least cleaned off the dead yellowed grass off of my face that was stuck on by my tears and sweat, so that was good. I found it odd how this young looking guy approached me. I think he pretended he had to throw away something in the trash or fake having to use the bathroom in order to get close enough to me so that it would qualify to his boss that he should help me. Sort of like, well, since I'm here, I could reach out a hand and help her. I'm really not sure. But he smiled briefly, sheepishly and told me he hoped I got well soon, but in a hushed voice as if risking to be found out by the others overhearing him, then risking being tortured by them later for his thoughtfulness and compassion towards me.

It took some time for help to arrive and I felt it surreal that here I was, badly injured, alone, unable to stand, walk or drive, without a way to contact anyone and my purse and contact information was way across the parking lot in my car. I was hungry. I was exhausted from being in the direct sun for hours, no shade, and no water. Here I was with no health insurance, sitting on a park bench with a mentally challenged park attendant who had been kind enough to get me a bag of ice for my knee. He sat and waited with me for some time, and just let me cry an cry and cry. He was so sweet, patient and loving. God bless him. I wanted to pray. I wanted to talk to a friend, to my parents, to anyone, but instead just sat and waited and appreciated the company I did have. Welcome to Los Angeles, Marcie. You are no longer in Kansas, Dorothy.

A Turkey Baster Was The Measure Of My Life

Inside the doctor's office next to the ER, I lay crumpled up in a ball on the bed, blood scrapes on my knees and elbows, dried sweat on my body and yellowed grass still in my hair, awaiting the results of my X-rays. In walked the doctor and for the most part at least he was personable which was a welcomed cry from the heartless group of jackals I had been around earlier, minus the PA guy who helped me then most likely got fired for doing so. The doctor began to explain how badly my knee was injured and I think at that point I somewhat blacked out. He lost me at, "It's pretty bad and you'll need surgery." I went numb. I think I began to cry again, wondering how there was any water left in my body at all at this point to muster the tears. I was really scared now. I wanted to vomit but didn't have the energy. I felt helpless. I had blown out my ACL and filleted my medial and lateral meniscus. It was a sprain too, to some other part but not sure how that measured up to what was now a hanging fringe of an ACL and functioning right knee altogether.

That was the overall list of the major injury to my right knee. The following list of minor injuries I couldn't bear to hear by that time. In the world of knees and good knee health, I was not in good standing, no pun intended. I was given two options, neither of which alleviated my intense nausea and feelings of devastation and fear. I felt like I went over that last hurdle and landed in a huge sinkhole. The doctor could, right then and there, perform a partial drainage of my knee to alleviate the massive swelling and pain, but the odds were very high it would again swell up to about the same size it was currently and probably overnight. My knee resembled a pregnant grapefruit and this grapefruit was having triplets. I was drunk with pain, and I may have even taken a pill or two given to me by a smiling nurse as I entered the hospital. At least I hope she was a nurse. Anyway, she offered, I accepted, no questions asked. I told the doctor to go ahead and drain my knee. I shouldn't have looked at that needle! But I did. Holy shit! It was like something out of a hybrid Frankenstein and Hitchcock movie. It was huge! My mind flashed to the needle used on my brother during his botched hip bone marrow draw. The syringe looked like a turkey baster. It may have been a turkey baster. It was near to the holidays. It was a turkey baster.

I covered my eyes with my hands and began to cry again. Here we go... In went the needle and out came a lot of fluids...*a lot,* until the doctor said, "Well, I could keep going, but now it's just blood I'm taking." He went on to say, "Oh and according to your records you don't currently have health insurance so you are not eligible for surgery." "I'm only able to administer the most basic medical care and nothing more." Through my pain, nausea and somewhat drug induced haze I thought that to be wrong. Not the medical insurance part because I understood that, but the other part. I needed my blood, right? So I said, "Stop! Leave my blood alone!" "I'm sure I need that!" "Remove the turkey baster!" Then he leaned in to my left side and said, "Do you want to see how much I was able to distract? It's quite a lot!" Mentally I gave him the middle finger and told him to rethink the length of his freakish eyebrows, but physically I motioned a polite 'no.'

Less Motion, Huge Change

A few days passed and I was sequestered for the most part to the couch in the living room where I was surrounded by a stack of books I had requested my friend David pick up for me at the local library. Since I was unable to walk or really stand for longer than a few minutes, no matter having crutches, it seemed a productive use of my time to try and educate myself on healing. I was for the most part not loopy on pain killers so I could actually focus and read rather coherently. And quite frankly, I had run out of options so anything at all about the study and possibility of self healing, and I was all ears. The books were centered around various types of healing modalities from the East and West, and writings about death and dying. Elizabeth Kubler-Ross wrote a book called, Death and Dying, and I got excited at the thought of talking with her or writing her a letter to let her know her life's studies on this subject had helped me begin to unravel some of my deeper inquiries into the subject regarding my brother. I was onto something and an actual person who may have some real answers was only living miles away in Arizona. Could this be her? Surely she could answer my burning questions! But, just as I got pen and paper ready, I find out she had passed earlier that same year, only about 5 months prior. *So close.*

I come across Dr. Edgar Cayce's book, Healing Miracles on the power of self healing through natural remedies from nature. I was intrigued. Of course nature was perfect and I was compelled to unveil all the hidden secrets nature held. This grabbed my attention a bit more than most of the other books. A doctor writing a book about how a person can systematically heal his or herself by taking various simple steps and incorporating nature's resources. Plus he was a bit of a rogue doctor, probably a rascal. I liked him already. I was game to try his remedies. It was a dip of my proverbial big toe into the waters of alternative healing, but it made sense to my mind that nature played a strong part in it. Duh. I tried a couple of his self healing processes and I got inspired! My right knee at the time of bedtime was a small blimp, but upon waking up the next morning, after I had applied one remedy to combat swelling, I found it worked and worked well. The swelling in my right knee had decreased by about 75%. I was onto something and felt a renewed sense of inspiration.

Over the next couple weeks I voraciously read other authors books on Angels, Intuition, and other similar self journey genres and insights. It wasn't like any light went off in my head, nor did I feel a huge epiphany over any of the information, but it felt comfortable.

I felt like I was swimming in familiar waters. Something felt very natural, in fact maybe so familiar it didn't catch my attention at first. It felt like I somehow *already knew* this stuff. *But how?* This to me was another epiphany. Hmmmm...

While recovering from my battered knee, I decided to become certified in Reiki and Polarity healing modalities, and looked into when the next classes would take place. I became a Reiki Master certified practitioner, as well as Level II polarity practitioner in a matter of a few months. Lickety split! I sniffed around at getting my degree in Chinese medicine or Reflexology certification, but nothing really grabbed at me strongly, enough, not even the Reiki or Polarity certifications. Inspired but dismayed by my certifications and accomplishments, I felt adrift yet again. Crap. Sigh....*now what?*

There is a saying that bad things come in threes. But sometimes they just keep coming, bypassing any known universal or spiritual law. Aside from my knee still being badly injured and not eligible for surgery without health insurance to properly repair it, with my money dwindling way too quickly, with my agency blacklisting me for fear that I would sue them over my knee injury, and the fact that I had only two training clients and no other income to speak of, I was in a bad way and for the first time I could not spring to my feet and get myself out of this one. Literally, I could not spring to my feet! I could hobble on one foot, but that was not going to cut it. I had been estranged from my roommates and forced to move out in one day in order to have my sanity and my personal safety intact. I remember crying myself to sleep more than a few nights, afraid and feeling helpless at what had become of my life in such a short time. There was no chance to reach out to my parents, either one of them, for fear of their heart stopping at hearing what I was facing. I was in my own sort of riches to rags story. But now, for the first time ever in my life, I was out of options. I was in the tightest corner possible. This was an uncomfortable and terrifying place to be.

Gas, Food or Lodging?

At 30 years old, I was living out in the valley with friends in exchange for fitness training. I had three part time jobs, a bad knee, and was barely making due. My daily budget was $7.00 a day, which meant I had to choose whether to eat or buy gas, since I had to drive from the valley to Hermosa Beach, then into LA, then back to the valley six days a week for work. I had lost weight and I am slight to begin with. I felt invisible and more of a burden than a help or an asset to anyone. It was difficult meeting new people and making friends but there was one person in particular who came into my life at this time who was like an angel. He spotted me while working behind the front desk of a local gym in Hermosa Beach, as one of my many jobs at the time, and we got to talking. It didn't hurt that he was brutally handsome. Turns out he was starting a new business and needed some part-time help. He had a captivating smile and chuckle, and he even enjoyed my verbal razzing and comedic bantering so he was ok in my book. He was a risk-taking, hard-working, wise-cracking, flip flop and shorts-no-matter-the-weather kind of character who was willing to take a risk at hiring me. He flew by the seat of his boxer shorts and I admired that. I remember my work desk was a door he had taken off it's hinges, and thinking to myself, *that's an actual door he* may *need for privacy's sake*, but no matter. We forged ahead and together we constructed my "office." He put me in charge of setting up the fax machine-copier-letter-opener-in-one gadget, which may have also been linked to his car alarm. But me set up anything that was electronic? Hilarious, because I am never the person others call on to do anything of that nature, just shy of helping open a bottle of wine. I could barely answer my phone successfully. Amazed at myself, I got it to work and we were off to the races. This was the time of the hit movie Jerry McGuire, and he was the epitome of Tom Cruise's character. Good times...

Eventually my being run down, still injured and working too many hours for barely any gain nor adequate sleep and nutrition, I became quite ill with walking pneumonia and a terrible sore throat. I couldn't afford medication nor a doctor's visit, so I remember taking a few aspirin and getting on with my survival. Even a visit to the free clinic to get the appropriate medications was not an option for fear I would be fired from taking time off from one of my multiple jobs. My family had no idea how bad things were for me, and since I was not terribly close to Mom at the time, the idea of calling her didn't inspire. Dad was not fond of me being in Los Angeles at all and had to resort to what he knew to do to cope with his own feelings. Tough love. This meant almost zero contact between us. My brothers were in no position to help so I didn't want to scare them or bother them with my challenges.

The inspiration and enthusiasm I had moved from Oregon to Los Angeles with, along with all of the possibilities being ripe for nothing but success, now felt ripped to shreds. I felt destroyed and rather pathetic. This realization of my life presented itself as such a mess, which I called "my life." It felt like barely living to me. The sheer magnitude of the pummeling I had faced in a very short time had taken its toll. I was a tough one but like a fighter that has taken too many hits, I could not find the stamina to spark any further inspiration. I felt cornered and dangerously close to the edge of a sheer cliff with a ravenous tiger coming from behind. I couldn't think of anything to pull me out of this. Had I had a propensity for heavy drugs, a reckless life, or prostitution, this would have been the golden moment to go down that road. But I couldn't afford loads of alcohol, I had never taken pills, and I hated the feeling of being drunk, so that option was out. And prostitution? Not even a chance.

The Book That Became My Soul Mate

Aside from my broken knee, I was a very healthy young woman and in the prime of my 31-year life, despite the cold, walking pneumonia, high fever, uncontrollable sweats, and exhaustion. When I couldn't see any way to help me out of this scary mess, as luck would have it, I reconnected with a friend in Los Angeles. I had helped her out of a jam when we lived in Portland, and now it was her turn to be my angel. She let me stay with her in her LA bungalow for next to nothing, and was the emotional support I desperately needed at the time. She listened to my plight and smiled. She shared her protein powder and sweet potatoes when I couldn't afford any food on my own. One day she came to visit and brought me a book and told me "read!" A book? *Why not a winning lottery ticket?* It was orange, rather thick and looked intimidating with all of the Indian references, spiritual dialogue and a strange and curious man's face on the front cover. I reluctantly mustered up the will power and took it with a smile.

The book was titled *Autobiography of a Yogi* by Paramhamsa Yogananda. I was in unchartered territory! She smiled heartfully and looked me in the eyes as she saw I accepted her gesture. I was feeling a combination of slight relief, confusion and annoyance all at once. I remember sleeping on a thin mat in her spare room underneath a window that couldn't be shut completely due to a botched paint job after the last renters had moved out. Already shivering with a fever and pneumonia, and crying a lot through my meager attempts to read this crazy novel, I tried to power through.I got through some parts easily and I remembered certain things very strongly jumping out at me, such as the recounting of an experience by Yogananda with Babaji, an immortal Divine Soul, and Babaji's sister. What struck me was the immortal part and also that his sister appeared out of the side of a mountain *as if that* was *normal,* for this gathering or meeting of souls if you will. Is the soul immortal? Wait…this was new information and I liked what I was learning. Well, then the soul has to go somewhere when a person dies. A light went off in my head as a I felt a current of inspiration. It felt strangely familiar, these profound "Indian experiences" and I wanted more. I read on.

Another part that stuck out was Paramhamsa's immense love and devotion and unbreakable bond for his mother and his guru. This was the first time I had heard the concept of 'guru' and I noticed I had no negative reaction to that kind of relationship, which surprised me. In another part of the book, Paramhamsa was in his hotel room and had learned his guru had taken final *samadhi*. But that same night, as if to be very natural, his guru appeared before him. It was a real occurrence referred to by Indian vernacular as Divine *darshan*. I was fascinated. Also incredibly, was the tale that when Yogananda was asked, in 1920, to travel to Boston to give a speech at the International Congress of Religious Liberals, on The Science of Religion, he knew not a word of English. However, he went into deep meditation just moments before going out on stage, and his guru let him know that all would be alright, that he would speak through Yogananda. His speech was articulate and elegantly given in perfect English. It was the very first bridge between Eastern and Western religions. I knew I wanted this in my life! I prayed for someone like this guru of Yogananda's to appear for me.

I read and re-read certain parts of the book and it became my solace, my new best friend. I would crawl into bed, sometimes coughing so long and hard I would dislodge a rib and break out in massive sweats, but when that fit would pass, wiping away the dampness on my face with the back of my hand, I would look deeply into Yogananda's eyes and just cry at what felt to be an overwhelming connection to this strange Indian dude I knew nothing about. Or did I? I would sleep curled up around this thick orange colored paperback and it felt as if like faint smoke creeping in through the window, the message of this poignant book seeped into me, awakening something in me, summoning and stirring up a deeper part of me, answering my longing for answers. I would dream about him and I would become annoyed to wake up, leaving my dreams with him behind. Later, learning the impactful significance of that little orange book and just who Paramhamsa was, and the *dharma* or soul's purpose he came to accomplish, I winced, recalling my remark and referral to him as "that Indian dude."

Marcie Anderson

Two Divine Souls, A Good Cry, And A Carnival

What could possibly be an amazing opening line to a joke, was in reality no joke at all. I felt consumed by a combination of sheer fear and the concern for my life and safety. I felt I had hit an actual dead end in my life, and I was even tired of feeling that. I needed a positive break or at least to change things up a bit. I decided to get away for a few hours. I felt a pent up primal scream ready to unleash and I had to get away from the city. I got into my car, trusting I had enough gas to get me to the Santa Monica pier and back. There was something about that particular stretch of the beach that soothed me. It was later in the afternoon and I thought a walk on the beach and a good cry might at least help me feel better. I didn't have a lot of options. I was not in a good place and there was no one to talk to about what I felt needed to be released in me. I have never been one to contemplate taking my own life, but this was as close to wishing a lightning bolt would strike me down in an instant as one can get. I got out of my car, and although I was not in any condition to walk along the soft sand with a bad knee, I didn't really give a shit. For the first time in quite some time, *I began to pray and pray hard*. I had never totally stopped praying and asking for help and guidance but this was the beginning of a full scale heavenly assault.

I began to walk at a slightly more brisk pace as I prayed. I became consumed by my negative, fearful thoughts that seemed to fiercely crash against my deep knowing that all would be alright, like the convergence of two wild unfriendly rivers. And as I tried to shut out the negative thoughts, I became more angry and scared for myself and my situation. I was wrestling with myself, my ego vs. my soul. My silent, internal prayers choked by my constricted sobs became slowly more vocal and not so choked off. Without concern for others hearing my terrified babble, my brisk walk turned into a jog, and my voice began to strain against the tears that came flying out of my eyes like water darts down my face. Why was this happening to me? I am a good person! What in the hell did I do to deserve such a shitty, hard life? WTF? And where was God when I needing him most? Again?! *Then it hit me.* This was another loop in this cycle of my life bringing me the opportunity to take a peek behind the proverbial curtain like in the Wizard of Oz. My thoughts were running at me at light speed, swirling around my head that took me into a vacuum like state, noticing this and just going with it.

I took a great risk to better my life, or so I thought, by moving to Los Angeles, and now I felt like I was being punished for it. But why?! Could God not hear me? Was I really being punished? Was it because I flipped off that nun many years ago? I had been praying for years and now I am in this critical state? Did I even matter to God? How come I couldn't feel Him with me? Where was my angel on the day I blew apart my knee? Do Angels get time off or something? What was the insanity of my life and why couldn't something *good* happen? It felt like something was running my life—like I was on a sort of negative autopilot. But why couldn't I turn it off? By now my jog turned into a sprint, my talking to God was a tirade of frantic yell-cry, and I demanded that God show Himself. I yelled out, "Show me *right now* that you hear me and you are here with me and don't answer me in some lame way like with a stupid pigeon feather floating down from the sky!" "I need something bigger, show me You are here right now, God damn it!"

Waiting To Exhale

That *very next second* changed my life on every level, imaginable and unimaginable. I saw with my own two eyes, the word "Footprints", and it went across my eyes like a reader board at a sporting event. I knew in a flash what that meant. It had great significance to me. That was message one, and I received it clearly. That would have been enough for me to know God was in the house. But there was more. God had to up the ante quite a bit from pigeon feather level in order to get through to me, and I had made that very clear. There is a prayer called, "Footprints in the Sand", and the basic explanation of it is that there is this man who is complaining and blaming Jesus that he only sees one set of footprints in the sand, and how could Jesus abandon him in his time of sadness and desperate need?

After this man blames and yells and whines to Jesus for leaving him in his time of need, Jesus doesn't react but speaks up and says as lovingly and compassionately as only Jesus can, "There were only one set of footprints because I have been carrying you all this way." That guy must have felt like an ass. What do you say to that? Nothing. Or you just clear your throat, smile and say, "thank you, Jesus!" I was being given a loving slap to my ego subtly through being shown this word as plain as day, "Footprints." But I couldn't say thank you yet. I felt like I was in a mind meld and I just kept my eyes wide open, feeling this was not over.

That second or two that held this experience seemed to stretch on for many. My previous tirade just moments before melted away and it felt as though everything in nature, even the sky was holding it's breath, just waiting for what was to hit next. Well, it hit alright and when it did I stopped dead in my tracks when the word Footprints faded off to one side and two tall male figures appeared and stood before me. Right in front of me only a couple feet away! *What was happening?!* I looked around slowly to see if anybody else was seeing what I was seeing, but also in a very careful way just in case anybody DID see what I was seeing so I could pretend I may have not seen it at all, as not to risk my own sanity. But also, I didn't want to look off and away from what I was seeing for fear they'd disappear! I widened and squinted my eyes to make sure they were wide open and fully functioning. No one was looking my way. It was like I was the only one experiencing a separate existence, while at the same time watching a scene in a movie that nobody else could access. Everyone else even somewhat near to me seemed to be in a different world all together, as if under remote control and in slow mo. As clear as day, I saw what I recognized to be two Divine Souls or Saints. One I clearly recognized. The other was an older looking man with a white beard, headscarf and long white robe standing to the right side of the other Divine Being. They were smiling, looking so lovingly and patiently, deliberately and directly into my eyes. It was as though they were waiting for me to get it, as if they were saying, *"...wait for it..."* Their eyes said it all. They had heard my tirade for sure and they wanted to let me know without a possible shadow of a doubt, that they had heard me. They had not appeared by chance and they were not Hollywood extras wandering the beach from the far off Carnival of the Pier. God was in the house. On the beach. Right in front of me.

I learned a few months later that the older looking male figure I saw that day on the beach was Shirdi Sai Baba, a very well known, incredibly powerful and greatly revered saint and Dattatreya avatar of India who had passed in 1918, and who was just beginning to find his way into the hearts and homes (and beaches) of many here in the West. He has multiple thousands of devotees throughout India and his presence felt to me more like a Grandfather unlike any other.

Both Divine Beings were light but not like a Star Trek hologram, by any means. They had an undeniably strong presence, and one of such incredible love and sweetness that I felt encompassed, supported, as if lightly floating in ecstasy. In the vedic texts and gitas of India, it is all too common the way Mother Divine is described. It would take four pages just to explain her stature, her hair, her skin, her lips, her complexion, her sari, her fragrance, her walk, her melodious voice, and so on. Now I have a much greater appreciation for such detail as written in the sacred spiritual texts of India, and as I now fumble through to convey the immensity of my experience, I ask you to understand that I felt such a wave of love like never before in my life, like the one coming at me from these Divine Souls. It's as if this love was able to take on a solid form. It was so strong. I couldn't speak at all. I felt like crying and laughing at the same time but no sound was coming out of me. I wasn't even sure I was breathing. I felt a great weakness in my legs but I was so strongly standing, absorbing this grand and other worldly exchange. I knew I was coherent and in my body and yet I felt completely outside of my body as if witnessing this 'me' as a version of me in the same moment and experience. *Nothing* mattered more than keeping my eye contact and connection with them. It felt as though every cell in my body was reignited and sucking this incredible love and energy, and I didn't want it to stop. I dared not blink for fear I'd miss something. Well, I didn't miss a thing, in fact, something happened to me so deeply and so discerning in that moment, ensuring that my soul received that pure, universal cosmic energy, and that my heart received a huge blast of light and divine love. Every layer of me received this blast! In those seconds, I had neither a care nor a problem in the world. Time again stood still. I loved this feeling! It was such a moment of bliss and perfection and I didn't want it to end! I wanted to run over to them, because it looked like they were about two feet in front of me, but I couldn't move my legs. I wanted to run and jump into their arms and hug them and say sorry for yelling at them, and to thank them for hearing me and feeling my pain, and thank them for coming to see me. Instead, I stood there frozen, crying out of sheer joy, giddiness and immense love.

What Goes Up Lands Hard

That experience was like being lifted into the air as if I were light as a feather drunk on the feelings of lustrous and profound love, then suddenly, like the flip of a switch, I snapped back into normal life, onto the hard ground, feeling heavy, sloppy and clumsy. I was back in the reality of this world, back to the reality of being on the beach and again began to feel the searing pain in my right knee. These Divine Souls vanished right in front of me just as clearly as they had appeared. As I slowly came out of that experience, checking to see if I was whole and breathing and coherent, which I was, I began to notice other people, their voices, their actions, other cars off in the distance, and seagulls scraping for leftovers out of the trash can nearby. Everything that had faded so quickly off into nothingness during those few magical moments those two Divine Souls were standing before me, now seemed to come to life again as if someone had waved a magic wand or pressed the play button, creating the flow of human existence to reboot from slow mo back to what was considered normal. Things and people slowly began to look familiar again, but now I couldn't help but think, *what was real about any of this?* Life around me seemed normal but I was far from that normal now. *Thank God.*

With the subtlety of having smelling salts waved under my nose, my awareness shifted abruptly and I noticed that my face and shirt were completely drenched in my tears. It was like a fire hose! Those were no normal tears. As layers of myself came back, much like a strong magnet attracts iron pieces to it, I couldn't help but notice the pace of my quiet mind begin to pick up speed. Something compelled me to glance behind me as if to carefully survey the area and as I did, I noticed a great distance where my footprints would have had to be from running in the sand. But another miracle appeared. There were no footprints for quite some distance behind me. None at all. Much like if I had been on rough ice and a Zamboni had come and magically smoothed out the rough parts to a glistening, frictionless surface. And for this moment in time, an entirely new set of things coming in threes had occurred. These three-events all compacted together in this short experience were the very three that became *my wake up call.* Together they were the lightning bolt I had wanted to strike me down and put me out of my misery. Instead this experience shook me, invigorated me and woke me up to my very core in such a way I couldn't have imagined possible. This was the lightning bolt that was the beginning to the deep healing and connection to God I had been longing for.

I took a few deep breaths and slowly turned towards the water's edge and noticed it was very near to sunset. I nervously looked around for any men carrying straight jackets headed in my direction, but I was good. The coast was clear, literally. I plopped down on the sand, making sure not to sit on old discarded bread crusts or garbage, and with a slightly shaky body, I tried to compose myself and recount what had just happened. I used my sleeves as the only partially dry part of my sweatshirt to wipe away my tears and runny nose, and I wished I had had a journal and pen with me so I could record the whole experience, not trusting my mind to remember it in full detail until I would reach what I called home. I looked at my knee, rubbed it and held it in my hands to try and get it to stop throbbing, then settled back to digest what had just happened.

I took a few deep breaths once again and felt the power of the sun's energy wash over me, enjoying the feeling of absorbing it and for the first time ever, *feeling at peace just being in the moment.* Wow. I don't think I had ever felt such silence and peace ever before in my life. The next and final thing that took place in this energy came suddenly and as crystal clear as if pre-scripted by my soul prior to my birth. Words came out of my mouth so perfectly it was as though I had waited all these years for this very moment to speak them. I remember saying to God, and as if I had a microphone, "Ok. Now that you have my attention and I have yours, please bring me someone who is alive and who can teach me what's really going on, and if you do, I promise to dedicate my life to sharing all I've learned with anyone who wants to know the Truth."

> *"This planet is one part a type of huge disturbance to you. How to avoid this planet's crazy vibrations? Are there any channels for that? The Sky mantra."*
>
> -Sri Kaleshwar

Sky Element Exercises

Silent Meditation

1. Prepare your Sacred Space by finding a quiet, peaceful place in nature, and by getting comfortable and cozy. For this particular meditation, it will be important to bring your

awareness to your surroundings. Give yourself a few minutes to feel yourself seated, to begin to hear the sounds in nature and to engage all of your senses to the infinite energy of the unbounded sky. Especially through connecting to the Sky Element in nature, your soul is attracting like a magnet the Angel energy.

2. Take five deep breaths and release completely. Breathe either through your nose or through your mouth, whichever is most comfortable and relaxing for you.

3. Bring your attention to noticing any subtle shifts in the wind, or a sudden appearance and sound of birds, and maybe if you notice baby whirlwinds take form around you like mini tornadoes.

4. Sit with your eyes closed for a moment to allow yourself to observe how you feel by what this chapter brought up for you. Compassionately keep in mind and have faith that from every *Crying Out to The Divine Source,* you have been heard and your soul cries have not gone unnoticed. Consider for a moment if the answer has not come to you, you may not have been ready to receive the Divine's message just yet. There are no failures, and there are no regrets. Please know this. You're good. You're here now doing this exercise and your soul is elated by it.

5. What is the lesson in the experience(s)? Where can you apply *forgiveness* to yourself and to others who were a part of your experience? Where can you find the *humor* in your experience? Where can you apply *love*?

Soul Journaling Exercise

Meditate comfortably outside. This can be by daylight or night. Connect deeply to the sky and visualize your body as a vessel or straw. As you *see* the energy you choose to release in this meditation leave your body, *see* the brightest white/silver light enter in through the top of your head and fill your entire body. This brilliant, divine energy is all around you. Bring your focus to drawing to you this limitless Sky energy to create both a deep purification and a powerful flooding in of new, positive vibrations. You may begin to feel a profound sense of Divine love, support and connectedness to source/creation after this process.

Once you are ready, begin your Sky Element Meditation by creating the intention that you are summoning the energy of the sky and you are meditating to it with your intentions. In the Indian tradition, it is believed that the sky is Lord Shiva, known as the 'destroyer' of creation. Lord Shiva is also "Bholo Shankara," the giver of wishes and desires. Bring the power of the Sky energy into your body and acknowledge your intentions to release any negative emotions and/or beliefs, and release any feelings of unworthiness. To balance this, imagine you are a beacon to call forth the Angels through your heart and soul. Whatever you have been through to have caused destructive emotions, it is time to let it all go. Call upon the perfect balance of nature, referred to by India's Shiva/Shakti energies; the unmanifest and the manifest; the Father and Mother energies combined. Trust that you are absolutely connected to Them because you are an aspect of Them, and all Five Elements are in you. Sit and open your heart to your Divine Parents, speak internally to Them, then sit in silence and see what comes to you.

Once you are ready, reach for your *Soul Journal* and write down anything and everything that came as a result of your meditation. Sometimes an image comes, sometimes numbers, sometimes a message, maybe even a shooting star or two! You may receive a reflection from nature in the form of a dream or from a thought that has magically popped into your head that is the exact answer or direction you were seeking. Have no expectations and no agenda from your meditation. Sometimes the messages or reflections from nature come hours or days later. Be patient and know that from your intention and attention in meditation, you will receive an answer.

You are welcome to repeat your Sky Element Meditation for as many days in a row as you feel you need in order to reach a feeling of self assurance or completion. Do not rush into the next chapter until you feel ready, but at the same time, stay on track with your *Soul Journey Process*, picking up the Water Element next.

> *"This is not the truth. Whatever we can't see*
> *with the eyes, that we have to see.*
> *Something I am not seeing, that I have to see clearly.*
> *That is the God."*

-Sri Kaleshwar

Chapter Four

Water Element

*"The master and the student relationship is immortal.
The bond is not only for this lifetime.
That bond is forever and ever, for many lifetimes."*

-Sri Kaleshwar

Happy Birthday To Me

I was now 32. It had now been a few months since my experience on the beach and as I walked into work one day, which was still one of my three jobs, I noticed a table where two men were seated. They were talking over their cappuccinos and lunch and I didn't care about their conversation much at all. What I noticed most was one of them was wearing a mala (meditation beads). With all niceties aside, I barged into their conversation head on and asked the one wearing the mala if he meditates. Jack's reply was a simple, "Yes, I do." Without reservation I scribbled down my name and number and said, "Please teach me how to meditate." Of course, the male ego being what it is, he thought my enthusiasm was sexual in nature. *Hell to the no.* That ship was not going to sail and, in fact, the wind was blowing in an opposite direction.

A few days later he called me and we set up a brief meeting so he could give me my own *mala* (prayer) beads and a *mantra*, a specialized combination of sounds perfected to create a specific divine or high frequency and vibration said to link directly to the soul. I arrived on time and found my way up the stairs to his apartment in Santa Monica, ironically only about a mile and a half from the pier, where I had my experience. I knocked on his door and he greeted me with a big smile. Three other guests were already seated in the living room. I walked into his place and my eyes shot right to a large image of Shirdi Sai Baba, one of the Divine Souls I had seen during my wakeup call on the beach! Wait…what?! I didn't say a word for fear he'd think I was a nutcase. I noticed my heart began to pound a bit faster in my chest. It turns out the very first mantra I was given was the only one Shirdi Sai Baba left behind in 1918, as he was taking *mahasamadhi* the act of consciously and intentionally leaving one's body at the time of final enlightenment. At this time, there was only one woman with Baba in his *dwarkamai* or final resting place, as he took his final last breaths, and her name was Lakshmibai. As Shirdi Sai Baba was leaving his body, he gave one mantra out loud to her. She received this sacred mantra, or Upadesh, as it is referred to in India. She heard it clearly and did an amazing job sharing it because it is all over India and not only plays throughout villages on loud speakers at Baba temples, but throughout India, in the homes of many hundreds of thousands of devotees who pray to Shirdi Baba and now in many parts of the West. We spent a couple hours in meditation, and before leaving, I notice another photo but this one is of a young looking and quite striking man with a huge infectious smile wearing a white outfit with a red scarf wrapped tightly around his head. There was something about *those eyes…*

Playing Peek-A-Boo With Shirdi Sai Baba

Back at my apartment, I tried my hand at this meditation and mantra thing. I had purchased my own mala and now, with my own mantra, sitting cross legged on my bed, I closed my eyes to allow the energy from the mantra to go to work on me. No big laundry list of things to do, just sit, close my eyes and say this mantra silently to myself while moving the mala beads through my thumb and middle fingers. Well go to work it did! As I continued to meditate over the next few weeks, I was compelled to journal after almost every time because things started happening to me. I began to feel sensations in my body, see visions in my *third eye*, some refer to this as the command center of the brain, and strangely, I felt more awake but beyond the physical body reality of being awake. I loved this energy! This was the exact feeling of connection to God/The Divine I desired years ago, but never felt. Now it had become activated and I soaked it up.

As I would sit down on my bed to meditate, I would set an intention or a goal for my meditation, much like as an athlete, I would visualize my race or game, then go out and kick ass. *Meditation is really no different,* so I took to it naturally. No, it wasn't like I was blissed out or that my mind was completely void of other thoughts and distractions, but I noticed if compared to a volume knob, the activity and noise of my mind was much, much less than before beginning my meditation practice. My meditation was very powerful, it seemed to weaken any and all other distractions, and I could see the results in my life in direct reflection form my practice almost immediately. *This got my attention.* The visions and sensations I experienced were from Shirdi Baba, and the messages were very strong and made sense, almost as if to show me a partial road map of my life, and each message and sensation referred directly back to a specific question and intention I had. This was a unique receiving of a download of remembering, but how did I know any of this?

I was literally having communication and interaction with this Divine Soul regarding the questions I had locked in me from the time I was seven years old. The beginning activation of such deep levels of clarity was taking hold. And it felt like this communication was not only for this lifetime, but also revealed past lives, and offered insights of future lifetimes. I was fully aware of the dual life I was living as I communicated with the Saint Shirdi Sai Baba in my little room, sitting on my Grandma's guest room hand me down bed with lumpy mattress and all in Los Angeles, with my one overhead light out and only my little bedside lamp straining to make a difference.

What was happening? Was this normal? I was seeing animated visions of Shirdi Baba in my third eye during my meditation. I had never had any of these experiences while sitting in the wooden pews on any given Sunday, dreaming of donuts and trying to cover my nose trying not to smell the stinky cologne the old brown polyester man sitting next to me had on. I was a little scared yet strangely excited and curious as I was having these moments with Shirdi Baba. I even remember laughing a few times at his playfulness. Meditation that makes you laugh? *I was all over this!* With no guide in my meditation practice, I had no idea whether this was normal or not. It's not like I had a coach. I didn't care. I loved my new meditation and took to it like a duck to water. I found myself playing with Baba in my meditations. I was giddy that I was actually having fun while meditating. What a concept! I'd close my two eyes, then I'd begin to see him in my third eye. I'd try to sneak open one eye to see if he'd still be there. Then I tried opening both of my eyes *really* fast then closing them again, thinking maybe I'd trick him. Silly me. For those of you reading this now who know anything of Shirdi Sai Baba, there is no tricking of him, but lots of him tricking you. Spiritual hide and seek was our game, and I was thrilled to play. I could not even come close to competing with him! White flag, He wins. *Always.*

The Nine Mantras Of The Five Elements

The next step for my personal meditation process and practice was to expand to the nine different mantras that are at the very core and the foundation of this Creation, of nature. These nine mantras make up the energy of The Five Elements; Earth, Fire, Sky, Water, and Air. There are three Earth mantras, one Fire, one Sky, one Water, and three Air in total, and each has its own diksha (energetic boundaries related to chanting each one consecutively without missing a day and the benefits thereof).

I began right away, leaving no room for excuses. This practice was like for the first time, being able to breathe the most pure air and it felt amazing. My life, my thoughts, my clients, my friends, my ability to feel and be grounded and in the moment, and my energy continued to change, to improve, to refine along with my confidence. A deep sense of Divine protection began to grow in me. I broke up with my boyfriend, I lost a job, but then gained new training clients, so I gained greater faith in the process. I began to trust in an entirely new way, and understood that what was supposed to fall away meant it was time for it to leave, shift, and that which appeared was meant to be right in that moment. I started with two Earth mantras right out of the shoot, and I can say, the Earth began to move for me! For the first time I was living my life in the reality of *Let Go, Let God, with no questions asked.* A feeling of strength and confidence grew in me that could be shared and implemented for the positive benefits of myself and my clients. I felt my awareness grow exponentially. I began to feel layers of being peaceful and satisfied for the very first time in my life. I was now beginning to experience an inner strength and a deeper connection to God that I had never known and I loved it! It was like I was the Incredible Hulk of Spirituality but I was not green, my teeth didn't turn yellow, and none of my clothes were torn up.

I had hit my stride in these mantras and ancient teachings of this Creation, not only because I could feel the connection to the Divine Energy, but because I am a practical character and if A + B = C and C is a positive thing, I'm in. And this was very clearly A + B = C. There was no promise of donuts after my meditations and for the first time, that was a good thing! This was another sort of epiphany. I noticed that nobody was telling me to meditate, or telling me that it would be good for me. I felt no sense of guilt or punishment for missing a day and having to start over so that I could complete the required 41 day cycle, or for wanting to meditate more in a single day. None of that. I wanted to meditate because I could feel the energy. I could feel a shift, a deep bliss, and a powerful connection to God I had never felt before. I saw and felt the results and that spoke volumes over anything I had been taught or shown before, and I remember the coaching Kaleshwar gave many times to his students. He helped us to understand it was important not to get confused, to know why you are doing a particular mantra or process. It was important each student have his or her own clarity and not to do our meditations to impress Kaleshwar, or because these are the recorded soul mechanisms of the Rishis and Maharishis, or even because Kaleshwar had personally tested them himself and found them to be exactly hitting the target. We were taught to experience them ourselves, then notice how our life would transform. I jumped in feet first and began The Five Elements process all on my own many months before I heard Kaleshwar say those words, so it was such a refreshing moment in my life when I actually heard them for the first time. By that time, I was well into my meditations and hitting my stride, secretly saying "weeeeeee!" in my mind the entire time.

"Spirituality is not convenient." This is a quote from my guru which I grew to love, experience first hand, and live on a daily basis. It was certainly true then, and still is. Because of the pace of my life, I had to plan out my days and weeks in advance in order to have 45-60 minutes to sit peacefully outdoors on my meditation blanket with my mala in my hand, my thumb in the earth, reciting the first two mantras I had learned, without breaking my peaceful meditation stride. It was awkward until it wasn't. At first I noticed myself feeling shy and vulnerable as I sat on the ground on my little blanket, careful not to place it on top of a fresh dog pile or puddle, facing the ocean right at the intersection of Ocean and Santa Monica Boulevard. This was not a peaceful cave off in India by any stretch of the imagination. People passed by and looked at me, then looked back at me curious at what I was doing, some snickering and making various comments under their breath. I noticed I didn't mentally flip them off. This was a good sign – I was making progress! Eventually,

all the dogs and people and various street noises faded into the background as I set my attention and intention on what mattered most, my practice. Even though my days were long and tiring, nothing was more important to me than my practice.

As the months passed, a fellow meditator informed me that the young Indian saint and spiritual master whom I had seen in the photo was going to be visiting Los Angeles. *I had to meet him.* I was nervous but really excited. What should I wear? How do I act in front of a saint? Are there going to be a bunch of freaks there? I didn't realize then the magnitude this meeting would play in my life. Nor did I comprehend how the past several months had been essential in my preparation to meet this Divine soul. The proverbial winds were about to change dramatically and with my open heart, faith, and inspiration as my wind sock, I was ready.

A Meeting Not By Chance

While driving to the home where I would come face to face with my guru, I felt a mixture of anticipation and excitement, but I also noticed an ease or grace that was becoming more familiar to me. As a young woman, living a fast-paced life in Oregon and now in Los Angeles, I was typically running from one thing to the next, but this day was different. I had left enough time to shower, pretty-up and change out of my work clothes, and had set out an outfit which made me feel a bit dressed up for the event, where normally I would be trying to change clothes while driving, arriving at my next event feeling a bit out of sorts. Traffic was magically light, and even parking close to the home was remarkably simple. Once inside the home, I easily breezed past others in the narrow hallway and found my way to the living room. I had no previous training in "saint etiquette" and was unsure of where to sit. Normally, I would sit near the back of the room, but was escorted by one of the coordinators to the front row. I relaxed into the moment as the room filled and the many voices became hushed as we began our first meditation in anticipation of Kaleshwar to enter the room.

At what seemed to be just a few minutes but turned out to be almost thirty, I felt a wave of energy very similar to what I had felt on the beach that day in Santa Monica in anticipation of laying my eyes on this amazing saint. Whoa, it was strong! The energy that filled the room was so sweet, yet so heavy, and resembled being tipsy without the embarrassing slurring of my words. I didn't want this visceral experience to end, but when I heard a voice coming from the chair in front of me, I felt pulled to see who it was. When I laid eyes on this slight, young smiling Saint, it felt like a vacuum sucked the air right out of me. I felt a magnetic connection. *A knowing.* A perfect knowing. But how was this possible? I came from Oregon and he came from India. What was it I knew? Why did he seem so familiar? Why did I feel like I already knew him?

It's hard to explain but the energy and the familiarity I felt in his presence was undeniable. He felt like family and it felt like I had been missing him for a very long time. I felt sweaty, I felt nervous, I felt my heart open and noticed tears forming rapidly in my eyes, and noticed my body got a shock of goose bumps. I fought with myself in my head, saying, "Don't cry, for *God's* sake, you'll freak him out!" I had momentarily lost my mind, or so it felt. To anyone sitting near me, I was cool, but inside I was completely spazzing out. Everything in my body wanted to jump up and hug him. It was an impulse that felt almost like a Mother hugging a child with whom she has not seen in a very long time. Thankfully the impulse passed quickly and I did not risk my front row position by getting body tackled and removed for physically accosting this young avatar. I took a deep breath. I had a quick pep talk with myself which went something like, "chill out and get it together!" Ok, good talk, message received. I settled back in to my previously calm state in order to listen to what he had to share. But I was not expecting what came next. His next sentence stung deep inside, as if a hot iron poker had seared my heart. He spoke clearly and with conviction, "I will not be on the planet very long…"

I felt a wave of hot tears re-emerge and realized I had stopped breathing. What?! I took a deep breath and heard myself scream in silent protest, "No!" I strained to grasp as he explained that he had only just started to learn English so he could teach his Western students the ancient knowledge and healing channels which he had been taught as a child by his guru. His guru? Then I notice, propped up in a large photo off to Kaleshwar's right shoulder, a photo of Shirdi Sai Baba. The saint whom I'd been playing with for the last several months during my meditations. Until now, I hadn't put two and two together, nor did I understand the bond between Kaleshwar and Shirdi Sai Baba. I found myself giddy, excited, and thirsting for what would be the next step in this curious, Divine adventure. I stared into Baba's eyes and communicated, "So *you* brought me here to meet Kaleshwar!"

Here sat this amazing Divine Soul from India. He had traveled here to the West to teach the West the East. I noticed I was drifting off, getting a bit lost in Shirdi Baba's photo and energy, so I did my best to pull myself back to what Kaleshwar was saying. I caught the points that seemed to resonate and seemed necessary for me, and all of his teachings coated in his strong divine energy were jewels. But all of a sudden he stopped talking all together. I looked around as gracefully as I could at the crowd to see who was the rude individual who had made this slender frame of a Saint stop his talk? I slowly peered around the room with my more mild tiger eyes, trying to lock onto the culprit, communicating through my eyes that I could give my full on ferocious tiger eyes in protest, but held back. When I looked back up front and into Kaleshwar's eyes after carefully scanning the crowd for the rogue heckler, I saw he was zeroed in on me! Holy Shit. I felt embarrassed. Confused. I wanted to disappear. I wished I had super possum powers and could just roll over playing dead so that that focus could be taken off of me. I had been the one to disturb him, but what did I do?

I sheepishly smiled at him and in my head was apologizing over and over again for something I knew I had done. Then an odd thing happened. He left my gaze and turned slowly to look up over his right shoulder at the rather large photo of Shirdi Baba, as if communicating with him for what seemed like two minutes. He held his gaze to Shirdi Baba's image so completely, as if he had to make sure to receive specific information from him correctly and exactly. He then turned back around to look right at me with this gigantic smile and asked, addressing the crowd, *"Who wants to come to India?"* My hand shot up before I knew it, as if my hand had a mind if it's own, and had been waiting for this very moment for years. Murmurs and laughter bubbled up through the crowd and broke the tension in the room. Whew! Kaleshwar, this young Saint and Spiritual Master of India, was hilarious. Even in his sincere attempts at heavily Indian coated English in order to share ancient teachings, I appreciated that not only was he extremely intelligent, but his comedic delivery impeccable! I appreciate those qualities in any average Joe, but in a Saint from India? I felt at ease in his presence. He was not at all pretentious. He was incredibly sweet, clear, humble, gracious, patient and thorough. Clearly he was on a Mission, *a Divine Mission* to share what he knew he came to teach with souls ready to learn, practice, study and experience, only to be able to pass them along to others sincerely seeking practices and tools that work, heal hearts, empower, awaken and change lives completely.

A Suitcase, A Long Journey And Some Miracles

I met Kaleshwar that night in May of 1999, and by July, just two months before my 33rd birthday, I found myself in southern India at Kaleshwar's ashram, if you could call it that. Construction had begun, and it was already at maximum capacity, with a few Indian staff and a handful of students, now awaiting approximately another 45-50 Western students for the Guru Purnima program. Guru Purnima, the festival of the Full Moon of the Guru is a time to connect to and honor the Divine lineage of gurus. It is a highly auspicious spiritual Indian festival which holds very strong energies conducive for meditation practice, personal process, and the exchange of ancient knowledge. Those nine days were an entire book just on their own, and I was elated I had brought along a large journal and a few pens in order to capture all I could.

I was committed mind, body, soul and consciousness. I had no idea what would be next in this journey, but knew without a doubt Kaleshwar was the one I had received that day on the beach in Santa Monica, as a result of my screamy-snotty-cry tirade, and that he would share with me and guide me to the answers to the burning questions that clung to my soul since I was that little girl knelt at the side of my brother's bed. But not only the answers, but the knowledge, the practices and studies I had prayed so fervently to receive and experience. Kaleshwar was my lightning bolt, my spiritual teacher, my guru. I was a blank slate. I was ready to learn, or more aptly, to remember, to wake up completely. This walking around in a daze was for the birds and I was over it. What seemed to be unchartered territory was not so foreign, after all. Kaleshwar would often say to his students, "It is not me who brought you here, it is him. Baba brought you here because he wants to see you and work with you. You are the lucky guys. You would not be here if your soul had not been here before."

Returning to work, to the pace and to the vibrations of Los Angeles, after such a journey, was just shy of torture. It was the actual Cinderella story lived in real time, minus the whole Prince Charming part. Over the next few years, I would check off the months and days in my calendar between my travel from Los Angeles to the ashram in India. I tried my best to maintain my business, and keep my clients happy, but it was impossible. I began to feel like I was cheating on myself, my clients and my teacher. I knew I had to study directly with Kaleshwar. I wanted to. Shortly after one of my visits to India, Kaleshwar came to visit his students in Los Angeles and give some teachings and sacred fire puja ceremonies. During a private conversation between just he and I, he asked me to come live and study with him and some of the other students at his ashram. He asked me what I was doing, and I knew he meant, "what the hell are you doing with your life?" But he would never speak like that. With a serious gaze, a firm tone, and a sweet smile on his lips, he said, "Is it really possible you can ride two horses?" I knew this was my invitation to dive deep into this knowledge and I recalled the sting of his words, *"I will not be on the planet long."* His words were very clear, and yet I felt myself take a deep breath in his presence. This deep breath was initially sprinkled in fear of what was to come, but deeply grounded in huge relief of being given this rare and unparalleled opportunity. My fear of what other people would think, including my own family was quickly overtaken by what I knew in my soul to be a huge part of the very purpose of my life. This meant getting myself settled in India and the sooner the better. Bring on the curry, mosquito repellant and chai!

I did not hesitate to walk away from my flourishing business with private clients, my successful modeling career, and my financial independence. Friends and family thought I was insane to make this decision, or had imagined I had been drugged by a cult leader. After all, how could I walk away from what had taken me over three years to rebuild, to live in India with a guru to throw it all away? In the prime of my life, my friends and family would ask me, "Don't you want to get married and have a family?" "You need to think about this seriously before you are left with nothing and no life!" "What security will you have in the future learning Indian things?" How will that help anyone back home?" "How will you make a living?" "Nobody cares about learning meditation." But the choice had been made long ago, before I came into this life. It was a choice on the soul level, a soul contract that I had willingly signed up for and to fulfill. I knew in my heart what I had to do.

Marcie Anderson

Washing the Dirty Laundry of My Ego

It was Christmas night 2001. I had fallen in love and was marrying a fellow student in front of our community, including Kaleshwar, many Brahmin priests, and our fellow students. It was a colorful Bollywood-esque marriage, minus the synchronized dancing and the multiple black mustached men, thank God because I am a bit of a wreckless one on the dance floor. I was happy to be married to a fellow student, and imagined a lifetime of devotional practices and service to our community. Magical, I thought! It was going to be just like in the Devi Bhagavatam, and Mahabharata.

However, the honeymoon was short lived. The bliss that came with getting married quickly turned to hell in a hand basket. It felt like I was riding along in a queen's carriage with my new husband, only to be tossed out unexpectedly on my ass into a mud puddle that one of the horses had just crapped in. I would now be entering a phase in my personal process Kaleshwar called, "washing your blocks." Wait a minute! I just got married. I was happy! This is what I wanted. *Or was it?* Going through this type of washing and purifying of wounding, the ego, and karmic patterns was not a walk in the park. It was painful. It sucked. I cried. A lot. I got fed up at my stupid blocks. A lot. I went like a mad yo-yo from anger to grief to feeling sorry for myself and sometimes a few times in one day. I was my own variety show of sorts in my head, minus the sequined cocktail dresses and too much make up-game show style. I thought to myself, what about this is spiritual? Over the next few weeks, my husband proclaimed he'd changed his mind and no longer wanted to be married and that he wanted me out of our apartment. In his mind, he was very clearly calling for a "time out" or a "do-over" like you would do when you were in grade school and playing nerf football in the street, only to call out these charges to your friends when a car was coming. With my few belongings in tow, I moved into a different apartment up two floors, but in the same building where my soon to be ex-husband lived. So 'awkward' and 'uncomfortable' also became my best friends in the months that followed. Chilled chamomile tea bags placed on my eyes to help combat my under eye puffiness from crying so much were laughable at best as a remedy to my appearance. My eyes and face felt like a balloon.

I was now more with myself than I had ever experienced and I stayed sequestered in my room for a very long time. Not like in a not-showering-or-shaving type of way like Tom Hanks' character in Castaway, and I did not name any of my pillows or anything, but I was heavy into it and committed to unraveling these layers of me that turned out not to be me at all. Well, not the real me, not the soul or consciousness me. My life was not going the way I had planned and I did not like it. And though it was one of the most compassionate and empowering gifts Kaleshwar presented to me over my many years of study and practice, I did not see it that way at the time. I mean, are you kidding? It felt awkward and painful and for the first time I could not run away or distract myself out of having to face the negative side of my ego blocks head on. My head was spinning, my stomach was in knots and my sleeping and eating became erratic at best.

I went through the process of first recognizing my own personal blocks, and then to how I thought about life, my patterning, then facing all of this as a whole. There I was in the thick of it, 'washing my blocks.' By blocks I mean the parts in me that I didn't like or want to admit to, such as: jealousy, anger, hatred, impatience, pessimism, feelings of unworthiness, emotional stinginess, having a broken heart, and fear. The "washing" meant first becoming aware of these shortcomings, and then releasing them in order to truly diminish their control over my thoughts and behavior. Then it dawned on me! This is what it meant to burn my karmas. This helped me see a signpost, a sort of finish line to this stage of my process I was in. And that meant raw, vulnerable sessions with myself, through meditation, and through studying the ancient knowledge. Cathartic yes, chock full of epiphanies. And epiphanies that I could then apply to my life to affect real change for the better. In order to process my blocks, I had to feel them fully. And in order to really slow down and hear my own beliefs and thoughts, I had to understand where they even came from. *Were they mine?* I had to buckle down and ride out this disturbing storm. I knew deep down I was being given the opportunity to release them in order to be become a pure, strong channel for future healing and teaching. Nobody wants to drink form a cup that's stained with 3-day old lipstick and rings from where the contents had been. Gross. I was in a process to become a clear vessel. The choice was clear but the ride that was washing my blocks proved to be uncomfortable, blistering, and beyond what I knew to be personal endurance.

Like a baptism of fire and water, my inner journey began. Kaleshwar's words played in my ears many times during my process. *"There is an exit in, but there is no exit out."* I was a competitive athlete by nature, with a strong conviction to accomplish my goals, to focus and dig deeper into my Divine faith. My blocks proved to be stubborn. But this time I didn't want out! I wanted to kick the crap out of my blocks and emerge the victor! My ego had other plans. It was under attack, and it fought back with all its might, sometimes taking cheap shots that took me by surprise. And when I felt most defeated, my faith waning, the power I felt from my meditations brought such a strong connection to the Divine, that my blocks could not be sustained any longer. This was purely an internal battle of ego, will, faith and determination, and I can say, it was one of the most grueling to withstand. The good news for you, is that it doesn't have to be a heavy weight boxing match like it was for me.

When we come into this world, we come as innocents. We are just tiny seeds, and our karmas and blocks and our conditioning have yet to hold power over us. However, seconds after we're born, the vibrations of illusion, and the duality of negative and positive begin their attack on our souls. Like a seed in the ground, in order to grow, our blocks need friction. Often conditions in our environment or the people in our life activate our blocks. The karmic positive and negative stimulation nourish the blocks and, in time, these seeds bloom and bear fruit. Sometimes it's delicious, amazing fruit and sometimes it's rotten and worm-ridden. Nonetheless, these seeds grow as we mature, and are conditioned either through positive attention or by the malnourishment of an unhealthy society, family, relationship, community, or all of the above. For example, I suffered through negative stimulation in my brief marriage, but had already obtained positive traction to purify my blocks and karmic patterns through meditation, by being in nature, and by becoming silent. Of course it didn't hurt being in the presence of a Divine Soul and high powered Saint, either.

I found the real treasure of my life to be the moment I began to hear my soul and could tap into my higher self. Once I was able to do this, I found all the answers I needed. In order to truly gain this treasure, I had to go through great effort. *"How long is it going to take?"* I would hear my impatient ego demand. *Then something opened up.* The struggle for me lay in the release of my blocks. If there is no attachment, there is no expectation to any outcome. And if there is no expectation, then all I had to do was just be, just meditate and observe, which in turn released energy and friction that was keeping me stuck in negative karmas, thinking and behavior. Once the attachments and expectations diminished, the suffering related to them was removed. I can't say the process of washing my blocks, with all of the tears and moments of feeling like I'd never make it through was like that of a waving of a magic wand, but when the moment of realization finally came, it felt like a snap of the fingers. It was up to me to let it all go, which meant I must relinquish my will power to the Divine. I was the one prolonging my suffering, with only my negative ego to blame. Like Dorothy in the Wizard of Oz, I had the power to go home at any time. I had been shown that I was in control all this time, but I didn't realize it. It was *the* Divine wake up call.

What a relief to know that I had no control over anyone else's feelings, ego, blocks or patterning and to realize this life was not about anyone's journey but my own. It may seem intuitive, but it is a far different thing to live through the entire process on your own and to come out the other side still in tact and even stronger than before. What came along with this realization was a huge wave of peace, clarity, humility, patience, confidence, forgiveness, compassion, love and healing. All the blocks I had suffered throughout my life had 'pouf!' disappeared. It felt like I had been holding my breath all these years and now I had finally and completely exhaled. In addition, and I would say to a larger extent, when I applied this 'new me' to all of what happened in my earlier years, I found such deep and profound love for all. I could apply this to my parents, my brothers, my teachers, neighbors, myself, and even to the nuns and priests who in the past ruffled my feathers to no end, and now had attained a real sense of completion and healing. I actually felt bad I had mentally flipped most of them off, maybe not the Brownie Lady, but the others, yes. They were just playing their role, as was I.

As if cataloguing the moments in my life, I began to peel away layers of beliefs regarding everything and everyone in my life up to this point. This was both a freeing and shaking process. I would dip my toe in this practice and through meditation and specific processes, greater truths about people, friendships, family, and myself, would be revealed. I would take my toe back out and need to recover and take a break from time to time to digest these paramount changes and shifts I was manifesting. Then it hit me. It was like a shockwave through my body. I realized I didn't really want to be married. *Wait, what?!* I smiled, then began to laugh at the suffering I had endured. I wanted to own that. And I did, for a long time. Something in me accepted the role of playing victim but that day, I fired myself from this role and never looked back. Once I had this deeper realization, and after many crying sessions with myself, I saw that I was not only going to be alright as a divorced woman, but that I had been given a gift; a greater depth of self, a stronger awareness and a sharp truth to what really mattered to me, versus what I had grown up to believe I needed to matter. There are a lot of 'shoulds' presented in life, and though I had begun my self-realization process through meditation, I continued to stack all of the 'shoulds' on my shoulders, while believing they were what I needed. This epiphany opened up an entirely new way of thinking, acting and being. This was the painful birthing of a new karma that came with such a rush and feeling of freedom, and I was thrilled!

It is difficult to receive a gift with your fists clenched. I felt like I had come out the other side of a huge transformation and now I had to catch my breath. I noticed I felt more solid, more clear, more at peace, more confident, more grounded, and more relaxed. I also noticed that I had never in my life felt this way before. It was exciting and unsettling all in one. If I had known I would have shifted in such a tremendous way by going through my journey to diminish all the negative qualities in me that ruled my life, my thoughts and my actions, I would have powered through much faster. But that's the rub. There can be no demanding of time. All I had to do was not give up. I no longer spun my wheels in directions that didn't serve me, so less likely to be diverted. My teacher would talk about '*Kala* (time). Kala does not care about your illusions and blocks and unnecessary attachments. Kala's job is to eat away your time and your life by diversion after diversion. It is up to you to wake up. Wake up!' This was the proverbial alarm clock set to high that I came to India to receive, and receive I did.

Feeling stronger, I enjoyed time spent in study, in meditation, in silence, in greater peace and in feeling settled. I enjoyed visiting with my friends. We would share our personal struggles of process, we'd gossip a little about meaningless stuff, and of course, we'd laugh a lot. Just as I began to hit my stride, and all seemed on track, I had a late night visitor. It was my estranged husband. There had been a lot of coercing, counseling and acts of kindness on his part to try and get on my good side again, and so I let him in. I think I must have sneezed that night, and in that one very brief moment, I got pregnant. It seems I had more lessons ahead of me! My world shifted rather quickly once again and now my head returned to its spinning. I was happy at the thought of becoming a mother, but truth be told,

I was scared. Different thoughts and scenarios raced through my mind, and it wasn't until I got a call from Kaleshwar, checking in on me and who was literally 400 feet away working in his office, and congratulating me, did my fear soften to trust, to love, and to faith. The water element switched from massive tears of ego wrestling and purification to my tummy, where Divine Creation engulfed me in a very different vibration of the water element, and where my little girl began growing inside of me.

> *"Once you can recognize yourself then you can recognize unbelievable divine souls in the universe."*
>
> -Sri Kaleshwar

Water Element Exercises

Silent Meditation

1. Prepare your Sacred Space by finding a quiet, peaceful place in your home. For this particular meditation, it is highly suggested that you either sit comfortably with your feet submerged in a basin of water, preferably up to your knees. If that is not possible, at least have your entire feet up to your ankles covered in water. You can add a few rose petals or even some pure rose water for this meditation, making sure the water is at a comfortable temperature.

2. Take five deep breaths and release completely. Breathe either through your nose or through your mouth, whichever is most comfortable and relaxing for you.

3. Bring your attention to any subtle feelings of tension or shifts in the body. Consider that this direct and conscious connection to the Water Element and helps to awaken the Mother Divine energy in you.

4. Sit with your eyes closed for a moment to allow yourself to observe how you feel by what this chapter brought up for you. Compassionately keep in mind and have faith that from every tear you have shed, either from joy or from pain, the Divine Mother has experienced with you, for everything you have gone through, She has been there. Allow the vibrational capacity of the Water Element to help you in this exercise.

5. What is the lesson in the experience(s)? Where can you apply *Forgiveness* to yourself and to others who were a part of your experience? Where can you find the *Humor* in your experience? Where can you apply *love*?

Soul Journaling Exercise

Meditate comfortably as your feet and/or legs are soaking in water. Connecting deeply to the water, visualize your body as a vessel. Recognize that since you are made up of mostly water, your vibrations are subtly merging with Mother's vibrations, like two streams coming together to form a serene body of water. As you *see* the energy you choose to release in this meditation leave through your feet, *see* the brightest white/silver light enter in through the top of your head and fill your body. This brilliant, divine energy is all around you. Draw into you this limitless Water energy in order to create both a deep purification, and a powerful flooding in of new, positive vibrations. Take this water deep into the center of each of your cells, your organs, your entire body. You may begin to feel a profound sense of Divine Mother's love, Her support and Her connectedness after this process.

When you are ready, begin your Water Element Meditation by creating the intention that you are summoning the energy of the Water. You are bringing your intentions to the Water. In the Indian tradition, it is believed that the Water is Mother Divine, known as the Creator aspect of nature. Relate directly this power of the Water energy into your body and your intentions to release and let go of negative emotions, sadness, and negative beliefs. Accept the idea that you are acting as a conductor through your heart and soul, and are calling the Divine Mother into your heart. Whatever you have been through in your life that has caused sadness or feelings of depression, it is time to let it all go. Call upon the Divine Mother as you would call upon your ideal vision of a mother, after experiencing some loss or great upset. Trust that you are absolutely connected to Her because you are an aspect of Her. Open your heart to your Divine Mother, speak internally to Her, cry if you must, then sit in silence and see what comes to you.

Once you are ready, reach for your *Soul Journal* and write down anything and everything that came as a result of your meditation. An image may come, sometimes a message, or you may receive a deep sense of cleansing and a letting go of that which you've been holding onto that has caused you sadness. You may receive a dream with a message specific to your intentions. Have no expectations and no agenda from your meditation. Sometimes the messages or reflections from nature come hours or days later. Be patient and know that from your intention and attention in meditation, you will receive an answer.

You are welcome to repeat your Water Element Meditation for as many days in a row as you feel you need in order to reach a feeling of self assurance or completion. Do not rush into the next chapter until you feel ready, but at the same time, stay on track with your *Soul Journey Process*, picking up the last and final Element, Air.

> *"Nature is the Divine Mother-Mata. Mother is the protector to make the soul (be) in the right way. God is the Divine Father-Pita. Father gives the light."*
>
> -Sri Kaleshwar

Chapter Five

Air Element

*"To win the master's heart is almost like winning
Mother Divine. I can consider it like that in my life.
It's not at all that easy."*

-Sri Kaleshwar

Bears, Boxsprings and Food Stamps

My pregnancy was a beautiful process of its own nature, and seemed
to go by rather quickly until the final month. I was ready to face this
new chapter of my life, but I was caught up in my head and not in
the moment. My teacher reassured me that everything would be fine
and that he was "taking care" of me. Those words, when he spoke
them, "You have won my heart. I am taking care, not to worry,"
were like the most melodious song and vibration to my heart. They
carried the weight of my experience, to a degree. They still do even
to this day.

I had good reason for my apprehension and unsteady excitement.
I had heard stories recounted to me about mom and her many
difficulties with pregnancy. Mom after giving birth to Brett and then
to me, had a longer recovery time than expected. The first episode
with Brett went misdiagnosed. However, when she was pregnant
with me, she was treated and stabilized almost immediately.

I had a nagging thought in the back of my mind – "am I going
to go nuts after I give birth?" Certainly I lacked stability in just

about every corner of my life. My marriage weak, I had no income or a means of earning one, and I had no real contact with my family for support. I knew I needed to be prepared to become a single mom. *This just got real.* I got to speak directly with Kaleshwar about my concerns, and like the most nurturing and loving friend, he addressed them one by one and promised me that my child and I would be fine and that he was taking care every angle. I felt buoyed up after my conversation with Kaleshwar. I had a few more concerns but each one Kaleshwar removed with such grace, healing and reassurance that now my only job was to go ahead and ride out this wave of pregnancy. Kaleshwar shared with me that my Mom and I did not share the same karma so not to worry at all about my pregnancy, delivery, or thereafter stating, "That is not your karma, don't worry."

He gave me a personal process to do which coincided with the monthly Full Moon and New Moon cycle during my entire pregnancy. It was a private meditation process guided by Kaleshwar that was only known between us. For the three days of each moon cycle I could not step outside of my room. I had a specific mantra to use in my meditation that was different from the Full Moon to the New Moon, and then once I gave birth the mantra process would cease. My meditation process added another layer of reassurance for me, and proved to strengthen the master-student relationship, which is an immortal bond. But now I was actively implementing ancient spiritual knowledge and mantra for very specific creation process and spiritual development of this soul I was growing in my body. A huge wave of peace and love came over me, much like the feeling of the depth of love I experienced that day on the beach in Santa Monica with the Divine Souls, Jesus and Shirdi Sai Baba. I felt at home with this process and although I had my cravings and morning sickness, they faded in comparison to this joy and excitement I had at being given to actively and clearly co-create a strong, clear, and capable soul.

I stayed at the ashram for many months and planned to give

birth in Bangalore. Though most of the hospitals and clinics could not compare to Western hospitals, I trusted in the process of this birth and knew after finally settling on one that provided a private birthing suite, functioning elevators and only a faint aroma of onions, I felt it would be perfect. So mentally dialing in to the last stages of preparation for my delivery, word came from Kaleshwar that we would be going back to the states so that I could give birth there. In my mind, the record scratched suddenly and loudly and I could hear myself say, *what?!* I think my heart stopped for awhile when I heard this! I began to run a plea for help in my mind that Kaleshwar had shared with his students many times before. It was completely appropriate for a time like this! He would say, "With your heart open, pray to me and Shirdi Baba, *"My dear master, you are my biggest well-wisher. Wherever I go, you are there. Make me recognize and experience this always."* My husband and I had no money, no car, no place to live, no income, no family support, no idea of where we were actually going, and we had no form of medical care in place for delivery in California. 'Ok Marcie, deep breath, deep breath', I repeated over and over in my head. This seemed insane, and as I came out of my mild shock, my focus went to my heartbeat, which was now faster and faster. What was I in store for now?

There were no options open to live with either my family or my husband's family back in California or Oregon, so we would move in with fellow students of Kaleshwar in Northern California. I knew nothing about their place but imagined it was off the beaten path a bit, where maybe I'd see a bunny scampering off the road or catch glimpse of a deer from time to time, but certainly nearby a town with medical care, grocery stores, and anything else I would need. Like fudgesicles. After having lived in southern India at the ashram where the nearest city, Bangalore, was three hours away, I was ready for a fifteen minute car ride to civilization to enjoy good coffee, fresh produce, and a manicurist. Not so! And while I am all for nature, peace and quiet, to have my closest neighbors actually be bears, rattlesnakes, mountain lions, coyotes, quail families, and scorpions was asking too much. Where was the MAC store? Where was the mall? I needed ice cream and a serious pedicure pronto!

I was well into my last trimester and we didn't even have a bed. We'd sleep on the floor on uneven box springs that were masterfully and tightly shoved together by the amount of layers of bedsheets to do the trick of holding them in place. I cried and meditated a lot over these weeks. I needed to see a doctor soon for a check up, but had no medical insurance. We barely had internet service, and none of us had any money. I looked hot wearing my husband's stained sort of white t-shirts and an ill fitting pair of sweats. We had been living in India and none of us were trust fund babies. I applied for and was accepted for medical insurance, food stamps, and a little bit extra per month for the basics. This fed and helped take care of the five of us for many months. Word got out fast that we needed some help and thank God for the loving neighbors and friends who would bring us bags of unsold foods from the local farmer's market each week. Eventually my husband and I were given a used car by his father so we could get to my medical appointments, and after sending out a heartfelt plea to nearby fellow students, we got an actual new bed given to us as a donation. Driving was inevitable since we lived about 3200 feet up a mountain, and we were an hour and a half away from my midwife and the hospital, but I had faith that when the time would come to give birth, everything would work out.

There was tension and strain between my dad and I and it seemed to build the longer I remained in India. Now back in the states and in need, I got up the courage and reached out to him for some temporary financial support. He chose tough love once again and denied any help whatsoever claiming that I had gotten myself into this mess and now I had to deal with it on my own. Point taken. My attempt to reach out to dad had failed and I hung the phone up in tears. Mom was not an option for help, due to her own impending nuptials. I sat on my new bed and looked heavily into the photo of my teacher, laser focused on his eyes and cried.

Relentless, nagging thoughts rushed through my mind as I tried to meditate. It was more difficult than I'd like to admit, even after all of the studies and practices I had been through, my thoughts drifted to all that I had sacrificed for my spiritual path. It was a scroll much like the one you would see in a Santa Claus movie. I felt like this was the dark cloud point in my spiritual process, and it came nipping wildly at the heels of my newfound peace I had just gained only a few months prior. How did I end up on food stamps, wearing my husband's long underwear for clothes and living out in the wild, miles away from what I knew to be 'life?' Kaleshwar would say, "It takes maximum pressure and squeezing to create the real diamond." It was one thing to be in India, in the presence of a saint like Kaleshwar, and go through intense processing, but now back in the states, ballooned up like a bloated Hippo, I felt squeezed like never before. I struggled to find peace and spent weeks wondering how I would come out on the other side of this one. I felt like cheap drug store cubic zirconia, all scratched up and faded, and nothing like the dazzling diamond Kaleshwar referred to.

I felt the baby kicking inside more often, both of us squeezed to our maximum discomfort. It was down to the wire, and I had been diligent and open-hearted in my meditation practice, ready to body tackle anyone that would get in the way or hinder my process. I would very soon become a new mother and I was ready. I could not deny that my marriage was failing and it had me feeling nervous and cagey, as if the pregnancy hormones, lack of sleep and waddling around in oversized mens clothing that was hanging off of me wasn't enough. I would run all the scenarios through my head of how it would be to be a single mom, if I would be back in India with the baby, how I would take care of my baby, and on and on. One of the most difficult challenges to my ego was fear, and I had to come face to face with it more than ever since I was now worried for two. But how could I worry when I remembered that Kaleshwar had told me, *"I am taking care. Do not worry."* I tried to blame my fear on my pregnancy hormones but I wasn't fooling myself at all. I had been to this particular rodeo before. I would go out into nature and take long walks and meditate. I would connect through the nature to my teacher, to India, to my confidence and peace. This was my solace. Through my connection to nature, to the Elements, and to my teacher, a process I knew as well as meditation, I began to feel my souls energy increase, and my fears decrease. In fact, that was a direct soul mechanism I learned from Kaleshwar; when your own personal desires are increasing, your soul capacity/peace is decreasing. I knew which side of the equation I wanted to be on.

A Babe In The Woods

I woke up one snowy Friday morning, feeling good, hopeful and rested. A powerful full moon and eclipse had just passed a couple days earlier, and the energy felt rather settled. As I made my way into the bathroom, having to relieve my now turtle sized bladder yet again, I noticed something felt different. A few days earlier, at my last visit to the midwife, she said if I hadn't given birth in this next week, she would have to induce. I didn't like the way that sounded and it didn't feel right that this birth should be forced by anyone or anything. This time, as I landed with a wince onto the cold toilet seat, I noticed some light pinkish blood and a very tight cramping in my lower tummy that would not go away, like that of a too tight hug from someone you barely know who doesn't know it's past time to let go, and now it's awkward. It felt like something was securely hugging my lower tummy but would not stop. My husband was at his desk preparing for a workshop he had planned to give over the weekend when I walked in and calmly said, "Remember the midwife talking about the symptoms I would have when it was time to have this baby?" "I just had all of them." "I think it's time." He jumped up as only an expecting Father would and said the unexpected. "Are you sure? Now? But I have a workshop to teach!" You can only *imagine* what was flashing through my mind at the time to verbally hurl back in reply, but instead just remained in the doorway calmly and smiled.

The drive down the mountain to the hospital was a blur. By now it was about 3.30pm, and I was pre-admitted into the birthing suite area into an outside room where I could be hooked up to a wall-sized monitor and gadgets and checked frequently by a nurse to make sure in fact, that I was going into labor. I overheard one nurse say to another, "I hope she can hold out because her birthing room is still occupied!" What? I had to wait my turn? I knew I was strong, but having to fight back against gravity and Mother Nature? Nobody mentioned this to me! I was not properly warmed up to have to perform multiple super human Kiegels! I would practice not only meditation, but seemed to improv an entirely new yoga posture in order to keep my baby inside as long as possible! I felt a slight wave of nervousness. I hoped the baby was hearing this conversation and would just do a few laps before diving off head first into the world as it so graciously and almost single handedly split my pelvis apart. My contractions resembled my personality; fast, strong, impatient and stubborn. The contractions would start, then spike, stay there, then ease a bit, but then repeat without much time in between, much like a full sprint to a slightly slower pace, then back to full sprint.

A friend swooped in to visit me in the monitoring room while my husband tried calling our teacher in India. He wanted to let our teacher know I was going into labor, but also wanted to ask if he should go teach his workshop or stay with me. My friend had come to cheer me on, being a mother of two grown children of her own, I appreciated a seasoned veteran to coach me through this. We talked and shared some laughs as she watched the monitors out of the corner of her eye. She knew I was at the starting line but the gun was about to go off any minute. I remember sitting up, feeling a bit queasy and feeling an intense need to pee, *again.* I had not been sitting up for more than a minute at the edge of the bed, when a big light pink splash of liquid came busting out from beneath my hideous hospital gown. Whoa! Now, more than ever, gravity was not my friend. For a brief second I had a flashback to a cocktail party and wondered if I just spilled my drink. Then I thought, how silly…I never did that. The effort it took just to stand up to go to the bathroom was challenging. Sitting down on the toilet was ok, but *oh my God*, getting up was tough. I thought, this isn't that bad, I can just have my baby right here, right? No. One moment I was in bed laughing and talking, and now I was dripping wet and being dragged down the hallway by my husband, toes curled under my feet like a sad rag doll, flashing everyone on our way to the birthing suite with my own personal 'full moon.'

The pain in my body increased as I stepped into the birthing room. I was told my usual midwife was not available. What?! What were with all of these last minute changes? This was not in my birthing plan! At least I made sure to put Shirdi Baba and Kaleshwar's photos on a table in the southwest of the room where I would be able to see them over my left shoulder. My teacher's words came to me and echoed in my now pounding head, "To be a true spiritual master, you have to be flexible and have a highly adjustable nature." What could I do? Nature was doing a fine job of adjusting me by now. I was in it full on and there was no reverse button.

My room was big and spacious. I had my own bathroom and shower, a rocking chair and of course a bed. The mini altar I had set up included some flowers I had brought, and I was happy I did. This altar was the only beauty in an otherwise drab, beige existence. I noticed there was a clock on the wall to my right and I took note of it. In walked a nurse and midwife team that were perfect. They had known each other and had paired up in births for many years, and once I learned of their reign and hundreds upon hundreds of team births, I felt a bit more at ease. These two were veterans and had claimed to have seen it all. Did they have trophies on display in their homes? They were so chummy I thought they'd break out in song or perhaps a cheer they had rehearsed over the years. But no. Now with my room set up and with dim lighting and the spiritual music of the 108 Names of the Divine Mother or *bhajan* playing in the background, I felt ready to hunker down for this marathon of birth. My husband was able to reach India and get the message back from our teacher that he should stay with me and not worry about the workshop. Kaleshwar promised he would tune in to my birth process via long distance meditation. *Sigh…thank God!* This made me feel better about what I was going to endure very shortly. The *bhajan* I chose for this process was one of the personal favorites of Kaleshwar. It was one of mine as well, and I made this to be another layer of connection between us.

I had a natural childbirth medical plan written up and highlighted to give to the nurse in full on Virgo manner, which meant well-written, very clear and underlined where I wished to strain important needs. I made it very clear that in the event I felt I needed drugs to assist with the pain, all I had to do was give a nod and we'd all be on the same page, much like signaling to your waiter for the evening, 'check please.' This was not the case. At about three quarters of the way into this natural childbirth process, I began to think not nice things about the nurse who had refused to administer 'a little something' to ease the pain. I would moan out my demand and she would breeze by me smiling saying, "Let's make sure you really need something. I will check back with you in a little bit." Then she'd magically vanish behind a curtain yet again as if she had short term memory loss and had forgotten who I was and what she was doing there. My contractions felt bionic. "Doesn't anyone care about my birthing plan?, I thought to myself. It's even highlighted, damn it! I felt an injustice and now my only focus was drugs. I bark-moaned to the nurse as I lay propped up against the wall in the shower, eyes rolling back in my head, just once more and finally she caved in, giving me a shot of something that slowed down my contractions. I sat with my head slumped forward, drooling on myself as the warm water covered my body in what looked like a meditation trance for what seemed to be about half an hour. I felt outside of my body. The drug quickly wore off and it was once more off to the races! I was helped off the bench and out of the shower feeling half dead, in numbing pain, but happy to have had this short recovery. I was coerced into the rocking chair. That lasted all of two minutes. Unfortunately, getting me in it took only a minute, but getting me *out* took about fifteen. Exhausted and cranky, I was positioned onto the bed and bided my time as gracefully as possible. But then came the medieval stirrups and I got nervous.

At the precipice of what was supposed to be one of the most joyous moments of a new mom's life, approached instead a glimpse into the reality and profound convergence that hit me like a bad stomach flu, and literally just before delivery. *I would be in this alone.* Don't get me wrong, my husband was by my side dong his best. This was something else, coming from deep down, a knowing. My brief insight was interrupted by the midwife calmly asking me, "I can see the head. Would you like me to place a mirror down there so you can see for yourself?" Wait, what? What kind of sick joke is that? "No, thank you," I said with shock and horror in my voice. The midwife, knowing all too well I was just about out of strength said to me strongly, "You've got some more pushing to do, now go!" I pleaded with her to leave me alone and to be quiet, mentally dismissing her to go out and take an iced tea break. But this of course fell on deaf ears because I didn't actually say it out loud. My last effort was to look over to my left at Shirdi Baba and Kaleshwar, pleading with them, "You guys push for me for God's sake, I can't push anymore!" A few final massive pushes later, where after I was sure I was split in half, my face red as a tomato, views popping out in my neck, and 'Ta-Da', my daughter was born! *A daughter!* The tears that came from my eyes sprang involuntarily as if on cue. They reminded me of the same tears I had drench me that day on the beach years ago. Kaleshwar didn't mention a Mother's tears at a time like this, at least not to my knowledge, but he did talk about the sheer potency of the quality of tears that a person can experience at the time of a Divine moment, such as Divine darshan. Those tears hold an entirely different and pure vibration. A flood of sensations came over me in milliseconds and my attention shifted to how I felt myself, after having gone through almost 9 hours of labor. I noticed this hanging, suspended and stillness to the energy around me that was familiar. It was as though I had been through my own death through giving birth. Time seemed different for a moment. It was surreal and coupled with the fact of still being physically connected to my newborn daughter, attached by umbilical cord. As if my head were on a swivel, I first looked at the clock on the wall to get the birth time, then looked over at my altar to both Shirdi Sai Baba and Swami, and gave them a huge smile, a thumbs up, and thanking them for pushing for me.

My daughter had come into this world at 2:12 a.m. on a Saturday. After the midwife coaxed my husband to help cut the cord, and as I looked away as he did so, the nurse immediately put my daughter on my belly, which surprised me, and snapped me back from what felt like a deep and distant floating meditation. My daughter who was now about 3 minutes old, lifted her head clear off of my stomach and with bright steel blue eyes wide open, smiled at me as if to say, "Great job Mom and hello there…I am so happy to finally put a face to your uterus!" I was utterly exhausted but caught the eye contact between the nurse and midwife when my daughter had done her new-to-this-life-gynmastics-display. Soon after they told me they had never seen something quite like that before in all of their years in practice. Ok, surely they both would break out in song for me now, right? No. I smiled back at my newborn. Already I loved her spunk, her character. I felt blessed. Seconds later as they forcefully pushed down on my stomach to make sure all of what was left inside of me would not remain inside, which was a painful and sudden shock, almost involuntarily wanting to kick them both from the evil stirrups I was settled in, they put my daughter on my right breast and she took to the colostrum with full confidence. I smiled and eventually drifted off to sleep.

Living away from India until my daughter grew to be about 13 months, was not an easy time. Many more challenges came into my life, almost too many to remember, and in addition to raising a newborn, my marriage went further into the crapper. Neither of us were happy, and I did not want to raise our daughter in a marriage and environment like I had as a child. Hell no. I knew I had to draw the line. Kaleshwar's words rang loudly in my mind, which was definitely not thinking nice or kind things towards my soon to be ex, but nonetheless I remembered the sheer magnitude and weight that negativity holds, so I grabbed for them strongly.

> *"Even if your boyfriend, your girlfriend, left you, bless them, be happy for them. Never ever think negatively on somebody. Whenever you start negative thinking on somebody, then the people start thinking negatively on you. It's a nature law."*

> – Sri Kaleswar

We returned to the ashram, he in his own room and me with our daughter in my own, we started very tense, awkward but proper divorce proceedings online. Since we were out of the country and would not return for some more years at this point, this was our only option. These brief meetings together with my soon to be ex were unwelcome to say the least. The fellow students we both knew who were welcoming us back, were in an awkward sort of live pin ball game state as they would see us separated not as a family, living in our own rooms. A lot of people were very confused to be honest and I did not have the smiles and the energy to explain anything to anyone. We would meet in a neutral office equipped with a working computer, and go through a rather long questionnaire to divide our lives. I've never much liked questionnaires and in this case, I felt stripped down to a "yes" or "no" as my future. In addition to these painful and graceless meetings for divorce proceedings, this was now crunch time at the ashram to graduate from the Soul University. This was the Olympics of the Olympics and I was going for all the gold medals in my studies. As far as my degree was concerned I had even more pressure to graduate with a degree in Eastern Psychology, which ensured certification of Teacher of Meditation, Ancient Spiritual Knowledge and Healer in Sai Shakti Healing techniques directly by the hand of Kaleshwar. This was a lofty degree to pursue and to obtain, and it mattered more to me than my own life. And now with studies increasing, sleep strained, and almost zero time for either in addition to caring for my daughter for the majority of the time, I was under incredible stress.

Counting Sheep While Sprinting

Post graduation, at the age of nearly forty, and with my daughter almost to the age of three, there was a short time period where things shifted gears and got back to more studies, meditation and process. But that time did not last long, which is consistent with being around a saint and master. There is not much time for rest. *Ever.* All of my years in intense physical training for competition and for the runway paled in comparison to the degree and level of training my teacher put me through. Seriously, nothing came close to the way of his teaching, and today I am profoundly grateful. Going through it, at the time, not so much. There was no under eye concealer made in India strong enough to cover my bluish under eye circles when Kaleshwar got us into process or intense studies.

Now the pace had quickened from a walk to a sprint. Kaleshwar was a master of all, but in particular a sneaky master of knowing how to push you way beyond your limits, both physically and mentally, all while continuing to inspire, with a smile and of course a good joke. He had such style. The year-long grinding of the ancient knowledge and soul level healing techniques just to graduate, in looking back, was only to condition me to crack wide open my own belief system of myself; my limitations and capacities. Far too many of us exist in a low ceiling reality until we are blessed by having someone in our lives to show us otherwise. The energy was palpable and at an all time high as far as the level of teachings and pace of which Kaleshwar gave his dharma talks. This was top of the mountain stuff, a much different stage, and it was not for the light hearted or impatient. Sleep was rare and good quality sleep was something I dreamt about, had

I actually been able to sleep long enough to dream about it. It was now becoming my teacher's sunset time, time for him to pass on, as he so eloquently would remind us. It was bittersweet to say the least.

A master at Kaleshwar's level has no fear of death, knowing that 'dropping the body', as he would refer to it, is only another illusion. "The soul has no death. It just keeps changing soul houses lifetime after lifetime." His energy changed a lot over the last 6 months to a year of his life, and so we learned to change, adjust, and adapt to him in order to keep up. This was not a time to miss your step. At one moment in a day, he would be smiling and laughing and teasing some students or his staff, then the next moment, he would be visibly agitated and impatient, giving a talk to the student kingdom, commanding on all of us to 'wake up, wake up, speed up, speed up!' The reason his energy changed was exactly as he predicted, knowing that once he attained the highest levels of Divine Energy Channels, nature would not accept him to remain alive in his body for very long. He was now avadhut, which meant he is a Divine Soul in his body, but his soul is activated primarily by his consciousness levels, appearing to be outside his body. To the naked eye, his behavior was odd and unpredictable but to the well-trained student of Kaleshwar, we knew this to be a phenomenal blessing. Kaleshwar would share about the lives of saints that came before him, spanning many thousands of years. He would talk and give examples of how each particular saint and master's energy and behavior changed and why. Kaleshwar was a living example of this bizarre and purely Divine metamorphosis, and he would make sure we were watching his every move. Everything was a teaching and now each moment was sped up so the awareness and assimilation of each teaching was like being a participant in a Celestial Pie Eating Contest. You had to keep your eye on the pie, on the master and keep eating, trusting the digestion was taken care of, all while remaining peaceful and open hearted, not forgetting to swallow. He was now clearly at these maximum soul capacity levels (for the body) and it came on rather quickly. The brilliance of Kaleshwar's teachings was that they were never meant to be only single level. They were multidimensional and multilayer at best, and as he continued to push us beyond what we believed were our limits, he would smile and remind us that someday soon our real connection to him would begin, and would be solely on the Consciousness level, where there are no limits. This meant that we would need to go beyond the attachment of being able to communicate with him in his body, face to face. It meant that we now had the tools and channels to communicate purely through our ability to access the silence and consciousness through meditation. It is referred to as the Brahma Consciousness, and it is beyond the mind because it is not about the mind, but about the soul and Higher Consciousness states. We learned that there are many different levels of Consciousness states as well. Absolutely when I felt I had crossed one finish line in one area of these vast and ancient teachings, and was just about to do my happy dance, there would appear many more finish lines. This was a calculated manner of how Kaleshwar taught; a perfect balance of inspiration met with hard work. Pushing beyond our pinched mind-thinking capacity usually when we were in Divine process, he'd magically show up with a smile, a joke or two, and a drum of fresh chai or a case of Coca Cola to keep us awake and inspired. Yes, some gave up, in fact most but not me. Of all my blocks I worked through to diminish down to specs, being stubborn I felt was a good block to have, when applied in a positive way. Happy dance time had arrived!

This was to be my last interaction with my beloved guru. After spending a grueling two and a half months in a meditation process as a member of a small group I was asked to be a part of, directed and guided throughout all hours of the day and night by Kaleshwar, one late night stood out in particular. I watched him approach the veranda where I had been camped out while taking part in this intense and continuous group process. It was near the very end of February 2012, and while standing outside the *dwarkamai*, the building where his body is now buried just beyond the temple at the ashram, he said to me with the most loving and heart-piercing look,

"Go back to your country, take care of your daughter's education, get her into a good school, and go do healings." I knew what this meant. There were no words for me to speak. *I couldn't speak.* I wanted to rush over to him and just hug him and not let go. I wanted to cry and say, "No, I can't leave your side!" But instead I just locked eyes with him, nodded as if my head was doing this on its own accord, until he was the one to break our eye lock and look away. I knew the depth of what this meant. The pit of my stomach felt alien, threatening, and hostile. The others standing around us seemed to feel the weight and reality of his words, and seemed to feel the gut punch to the heart I felt. I could only stand there looking back at him, saying in my heart, "Please don't have me and my daughter leave you now, not at this time!" I felt like this was the worst 'getting voted off the island' torture ever. But of course I didn't speak a word. I trusted Kaleshwar implicitly and I knew he knew what was brewing. I didn't want that moment to end. I felt like I couldn't move from where I was standing and I wasn't sure I was breathing. I didn't want to break his gaze and I wished I had the power to freeze time. He knew very well the physical and verbal battle I was going through. He gave one last compassionate yet powerful confirmation through his eyes right into mine, making sure I understood what he was saying and why at that very moment. He gently turned away and quickly got onto another important matter at hand, discussing something with other students. I knew this is what he had to do and how he had to do it.

> *"Before we take off (pass on), to see the real illusion happening in front of you, it breaks your belief system, the very karma of your illusion."*
>
> -Sri Kaleshwar

Last Call

My daughter and I made several trips back and forth in the final years Kaleshwar was living. She and I returned to India in September of 2011, after having been back in the states for about a year prior. Kaleshwar told me he wanted to work deeply with me and my daughter, and return to India as soon as we could. To my friends, family and clients, this was a tremendous leap of faith to once again, after re-establishing my life from next to nothing, give it all away and return to India. This was certainly a way of weeding out those who believed I was nuts. My phone contacts diminished tremendously. Again. Personal belongings sold or given away, our preparation for a long stay again in India was cut shorter than we could have known, and our life put on hold for the most part, my daughter and I arrived back to Northern California with only two suitcases to our name, having arrived in India with only four. It was just five and a half months after moving, having anticipated staying two or more years. We had not been back for more than 12 days when we got the news that Kaleshwar had taken *mahasamadhi*. He had left his body just a few weeks after turning 38 years old. We had gotten the news from India in late evening, roughly six hours earlier, to begin performing an *abishek*. We knew what this meant. It is a holy washing or bath performed to a deity statue to bring high, holy vibrations to a person, place or thing, and to remove suffering and negativity from the situation, and to create powerful Divine protection circles (soul strength). I continued the *abishek* for many hours to the Dattatreya statue in the Laytonville Healing Center and Temple as an offering of pure love and devotion directed entirely and with full force at Kaleshwar. I was the only one who could perform this special *abishek* because my daughter was too young and too tired, and my dear friend and her daughter were not well enough to help me. I remember all of us sang out a specific mantra during these many, many hours of constant *abishek*, the *Shakti Gayatri,* and by now I was starting to get dizzy and exhausted, almost hanging off one of the arms of the statue as I continued this loving process without stopping. I felt the energy during this *abishek* shift at one point and I knew in my heart Kaleshwar had passed even before we got word from India. I knew this particular quality of energy, and although gloriously sweet and pure, it was unwelcome. Similar to when my brother passed, and again when I had my awakening on the beach in Santa Monica, to then while giving birth to my daughter, and now again when my beloved teacher was passing-all the same quality of energy. I was aware to the reality of another experience of time playing with me. My teachers passing was a combination of a real life, a real time moment but coated in pure illusion. I was boxing with my mind, "it hapened, he's gone...no way, this is another test... he will be back." It was a feeling of being in a vat of honey and trying to powerfully swim my way out but I didn't have enough energy to swim out and yet I knew I could not give up or I would go under. I had to keep going. It was Divine, but surreal.

Kaleshwar's words, teachings, and predictions sunk into my heart and gut like a sickness. There began a pain inside of me that he talked about many, many times during his years of teaching, and now my understanding of his pain melded into mine. Everyday life for many months became more dull, mundane. I was going through the motions for sure, and yet I knew the tremendous dharma that lay before me. This was no time to curl up in a ball and unplug. Beyond my many years of dedicated study and practice, this was now a time like being called up from the minor leagues. Let the games begin. Kaleshwar's real pain in his life was that he never had his master in this lifetime in the body. Shirdi Sai Baba passed in 1918. Kaleshwar would often say, "You don't know how lucky you guys are to have me (sitting) in this chair", as he would gently hit the left or right arm of his chair in the *mandir* temple, while talking with us. He would look back over his left shoulder to the huge marble *murthi* or statue of his guru, Shirdi Baba, then he would say, "But someday you will know the pain of what it is like to not have your guru in the body." "You will know the value of this chair after I'm gone."

My mind went to this moment, replaying Kaleshwar's words like a cassette tape, taking myself back to India and back to his chair in my mind. Now my only connection to my teacher would be mostly through the Air Element, the Consciousness Level as he told us would be the case after he left the planet.

Not a day goes by that I don't miss him, his laughter, his jokes, his mannerisms, his grace, his stamina, and his sweet, patient yet strong voice. He was such a sound commander balanced by the depth and greatness of his selflessness, tireless hard work and love. I never knew such a depth of love, compassion, patience, forgiveness, discipline, knowledge and relentless, almost laser like positivity in one person. I never dreamt it was possible for one human body to encompass all that he was, and accomplish all that he had in such a short time. Really, what he did and what he came to do and share in this lifetime had *never* been done before by any saint. Never. The karmas he took and the karmas we were carrying were insurmountable. He took care of humanity around him and showed us the same path of how to conduct our lives. Kaleshwar would often say, "Spirituality isn't convenient." On my worst days, I know I am connected to my teacher on the soul level and the consciousness levels, on the heart level, and through memories of being with him. On my worst days, I know I can help share that love and healing and connection with others. Bad hair days aside, my worst days are very, very few.

Just to watch him at a distance was a gift. He was always working even when his human body was way past needing rest, a hot shower or a healthy meal. He was constantly and deeply connecting through his meditations and channels to the souls of humans, the Five Elements, animals and Divine Souls who had come before him. Sitting in his chair swing one time out by his Hanuman statue and fire pit, in this one instance, he slowed his pace and connected to a monkey clan where a baby had just died. All of the other monkeys would cry and gather around to grieve and bond and process the death and this lasted quite a long time. Kaleshwar would seem a million miles away at times like these. Sometimes with a tear in his eye, he'd talk about how once humans could treat each other with the same care, thoughtfulness, and love that animals in nature do, then there would be a real shift back to peace, compassion, and healing returned to this planet. There would be born a whole new age and time on the planet. Currently, obviously, this is not the case. But there has been a shift towards this positive, loving change and hey, it's a start in the right direction. It's a bit sickening to think about, really, that animals in nature treat one another with more compassion, love and kindness than humans do towards each other. I learned that to be born as a human is the highest gift. Only by being human do we have the capacity to reach God, to find the answers to the deeper questions about life, and to implement that knowledge to help and serve others, and to reach pure enlightenment. And yet the way most humans interact is uninspiring, shameful, gross. It is one thing to be able to receive, but is truly another thing to give. Helping others is not convenient, it does not care what time of day or night, it doesn't care if you're having a severe wardrobe challenge, and it does not care what is happening in your life. It is selfless service, or *seva* as it's called in India. Kaleshwar would remind us that the difference between an average human and a saint, is that a normal human thinks of him or herself 90% of the time, while a saint is thinking of helping others 90%, and only 10% on themselves. Sobering yet true.

Kaleshwar was a saint, an avatar, a spiritual master, a teacher, a brother, an uncle, a father, a comedian, a philanthropist and a best friend to me. I look at his picture more than a dozen times each day and continuously hold my own conversations with him. *I know he is with me.* I know he is listening. Always. And I know our soul connection and our connection on the consciousness levels is immortal. It gives me solace to know he could only have passed *knowing* he had accomplished the insurmountable task of his dharma. In his final weeks, he shared with his remaining students, "I am with you guys. I will not leave this physical body or this chair until I have given you everything you need. After that, I am a free bird. You will need to connect with me on the consciousness levels to do your duty. *It's time to wake up.* Wake up, help relieve and heal the suffering on the planet. Get to work."

> *"Try to see the globe like one bowl. Don't divide it into different pieces and in different parts. We're all unity. We are humanity. We need to create the peace. All religions are One."*

-Sri Kaleshwar

Air Element

Silent Meditation

1. Prepare your sacred space by finding a quiet, peaceful place, either in your home or outdoors. Be sure it is a place where you feel expansive. For this particular meditation, set your mind free to allow for an idea to happen, like a flash, almost like a bolt of lightning. Our intentions have no boundaries, so this can be an impulse to call your distant friend. You have connected in the air. Suddenly your phone rings and it is the very friend you had imagined. The Air Element makes distance healing possible.

2. Take five deep breaths and release completely. Breathe either through your nose or through your mouth, whichever is most comfortable and relaxing for you.

3. Bring your attention to any subtle shifts in your body or tension you may be holding. Consider that this direct and conscious connection to the Air Element helps to awaken the Higher Consciousness energy in you, and helps to balance and calm the "monkey mind."

4. Sit with your eyes closed for a moment to allow yourself to observe how you feel by what this chapter brought up for

you. Patiently keep in mind and have faith that from every *Thought or Intention* you have had that was coming from a place of wanting to feel deeply connected to Source, the influence of a stronger soul connection to the Air Element will make this possible. Allow the vibrational capacity of the Air Element to help you in this exercise.

5. What is the lesson in the experience(s)? Where can you apply *forgiveness* to yourself and to others who were a part of your experience? Where can you find *humor* in your experience? Where can you apply *love*?

Air Element Soul Journaling Exercise

Meditate comfortably as you sit on the ground with a towel or blanket between you and a direct contact with the ground. You may sit in a chair if that is most comfortable for your body. Visualize your body as a vessel or funnel that is merging with the vibrations of the Air. As you *see* the energy you choose to release in this meditation leave out your head and forehead, *see* the brightest white/silver light enter back in through the top of your head and forehead and let it fill your entire body. This brilliant, divine energy is all around you. Let your focus draw you into this limitless Air Energy to create both a deep purification and a powerful rushing in of new, positive vibrations. Take this Air Energy deep into the center of your forehead, to the 'third eye' or *Trineytra Chakra, or Gurusthan* as it is called in India.

When you are ready, begin your Air Element Meditation by creating the intention to summon the energy of the air. In the Indian tradition, the air or *Vayu* is known as an aspect of Lord Hanuman., and represents not only pure *bhakti* or spiritual devotion, but is also called upon to conquer the 'monkey mind,' leading practitioners to success in their spiritual practice. Hanuman also represents victory. Relate directly to the power of the Air energy and your intentions to release and let go of negative emotions, negative beliefs, and the inability to open your heart deeply. Unfortunately, there is a belief here in the West that to surrender to the Divine means you are weak. Quite to the contrary! True, pure open-hearted devotion to the Divine gives unparalleled strength and a newfound fluidity to spiritual life. Whatever you have been through to cause sadness or feelings of "bumpiness," it is time to let it all go. Much like the Sky Element, the Air Element carries the Angel energy. Open your heart to the Divine, then sit in silence and see what comes to you.

Once you feel complete, reach for your *Soul Journal* and write down anything and everything that came as a result of your meditation. An image may come, a message, or you may receive a deep sense of cleansing and letting go of that which you've been holding onto that has caused you unease and dissatisfaction. You may receive a dream with a message specific to your intentions. Have no expectations and no agenda from your meditation. Sometimes the messages or reflections from nature come hours or days later. Be patient, relaxed, and know that from your intention and attention in meditation, you will receive an answer.

You are welcome to repeat your Air Element Meditation for as many days in a row as you feel you need in order to reach a feeling of self assurance or completion. Stay on track with your *Soul Journey Process*, perhaps revisiting all of the Five Elements over the next few weeks to see what shifts, changes and inspirations have come as a result of your repeated exercises, meditations and journaling.

Summary

*"Start the day with positive, lead the day with positive.
End the day with positive, sleep the night with positive.
Wake up with the positive."*

-Sri Kaleshwar

After many weeks of writing, remembering, going deep into meditation and then opening myself up to how this book was going to be written, there was a huge wave of all of the events and emotions related to them coming at me, as you can imagine. But it gave me a chance to deeply reflect on what I needed to share and how to share it in order to act as a bridge to help assist your process of awakening, purification and healing.

It is my hope and prayer that having read this book, you also allowed yourself to remember pivotal moments in your life. Those that were seemingly magical and those that were challenging, creating the course of your life as it is today. That you gave yourself the room to laugh and cry and heal. I hope you can now see them as the great gifts they were intended to be. I hope you allowed yourself to be vulnerable and transparent in reading this book, and that it conjured up hidden inspirations and deeper truths that you can now face, because it is a part of your greater purpose and personal journey.

It is in the darkest shadows where we can emerge our most courageous. It is from the darkest night, that the most stunning sunrise is experienced. It is when the pressure gets too great that laughter can be the only remedy. It is neither wise nor healthy to hide our emotions and experiences deep within, so bring it!

I hope many questions and a deeper curiosity arose in you and that you know there are some answers. Real answers. I hope that you have or will find gratitude and humble unconditional love for your own Mother, knowing that no matter what your relationship, she loves you so deeply. If she is no longer on this planet, know that she loved you with every cell and with every heartbeat given to her. She did her best. Love your Father, he too did he is best. I hope that you have shed the layers of shame, guilt or unworthiness that you learned to take on, thinking it was "you." I hope that you laughed, cried, and took yourself out into the silence and healing of nature. I hope that you did something different, like wear your shirt inside out in public and took notice to how many people noticed. I hope that you will continue to strengthen your bond with nature and silence. I hope that you have greater clarity to your relationship with nature, the Five Elements, and with the Divine Mother and Father. I hope that through that deep connection or re-connection to nature, and to Source, you realize there can only be non-judgment, true forgiveness, peace, bliss, and an unconditional love for all living things and beings. That includes you! And last, I hope so much that you see now that you are a divine spark of this entire Creation, you can inspire others and in that spark, you can do the real wonders. The sky is the limit, and with the sky, there is no limit.

> *"Once you charged your soul it means the channel link has happened. The Divine force is linked to you. It's a standard law."*

> -Sri Kaleshwar

Printed in the United States
By Bookmasters